CHAMPION'S MENTAL EDGE

Turning Winners into Champions

ROBERT ANDREWS

ISBN-13: **978-0-9995337-0-3**

ACKNOWLEDGMENTS

I am thankful, and filled with gratitude for my amazing, remarkable and supportive wife, **Gisele.** I am grateful that you said "yes" to this wild vision that I had for our lives. You have celebrated the best of times with me. You have supported me through the struggles and times of doubt that I was doing the right thing or things didn't go as planned. It has been a remarkable journey. There is no telling how many thousands of times you have listened to me as I processed my experiences, successes, and struggles in my work with athletes, teams, and organizations. You have been supportive when I needed support, and challenged me when I needed to be challenged. I am grateful for your love and encouragement.

To our children, **Galen and Abby,** you have been my greatest treasures in life. You are caring, humble, heart centered, and have tremendous passion for your lives at such a young age. Sharing this journey with you has been a gift. We have traveled the world together on this amazing adventure. Thank you for riding along. Watching each of you in your respective sport has made for a rich and rewarding twenty plus years.

My father, **Dr. Robert Andrews**, was a gifted Chiropractor who started his practice during what I call the "dark ages" of chiropractic. He had to endure the ridicule of many who thought his approach to wellness was wrong. You taught me to continue to press forward as I strived to change the perception of mental training. You inspired me to overcome obstacles and take these struggles as challenges. You inspired me to live passionately in a field that allows me to make a difference in the lives of every athlete, coach and parent I am blessed to work with.

Simone Biles, and her coach Aimee Boorman, Laurie Hernandez and her coach Maggie Haney. For many years I have been the guy behind the curtain. I worked quietly behind the scenes to help athletes reach their peak potential. Each of you has been vocal and courageously vulnerable about our work together. Your openness to ESPNW, Texas Monthly Magazine, The LA Times, The Wall Street Journal, The Washington Post, and Simone, your book, has not only helped take my business to new heights, it has helped change the perception of sports performance psychology. You made it safe and acceptable for athletes to explore their mind and their emotions as it impacts performance. I am grateful to each of you.

Raj Bhavsar, Sean Townsend, Sean Golden, Justin Laury. You guys trusted me to guide, teach, and mentor you in the early phases of my work in the sport of gymnastics. I could not have asked for a better group of young men to work with. You were my introduction to the sport. In addition to being Olympians, World Champions, and World Team members, you are remarkable young men who are making a difference in the sport by being the right kind of coach. I am forever grateful to know each of you and have the depth of connection and friendship we have had all these years. Your support of my passion and work in the world of sports is appreciated.

Steve Van Meter. Steve, you listened to my vision all those years ago. You got it! In fact you referred me my first athlete. I am grateful for your support and feedback all these years. As a high school athletic director and head football coach, your insight and feedback has been incredibly valuable to me in this process. You have been and always will be a lifelong friend.

Matt Taylor We have been friends since we were three years old. I learned a lot about character and commitment by watching you as an athlete, a man, a father, and as a special agent with the FBI. We have always been there for each other and your support over all these years means the world to me.

Eliot Rose. Eliot, you were such an important supporter

to me in the early days and continue to be that every day that I continue on this journey. Our Memorial Park walks helped me sort out and process so many important details and components of my vision. You have been there for the amazing highs and the struggles I have endured as I built my business and my vision. Sometimes you have gotten more excited than I have when I shared great news with you. Most of all I cherish our friendship.

Dave Juszczyk From the first time I met you at the USA National Team Camps, we clicked. We saw things the same way. Our passion for the sport of gymnastics was the foundation of what will be a lifelong friendship. We have aligned to create a vision for what our great sport can be. You have been a rock for me during the toughest times of this process. Your wisdom and brilliance has been a guiding force in the creation and expansion of my passion in sports and my business model.

Dennis McGough, Becky Ewing, and Wendy VanWormer of Growth Coaching Systems. I want to thank each of you for helping me create the Champion's Mental Edge book and video series. Your brilliance in web design, marketing, and selling is unsurpassed. Dennis, you have been a powerful business mentor for me.

Javeon Butler of JL Media, I am grateful that you saw the vision as clearly as I did and connected all of us for this project. Who would have thought that from an initial interview, we would have ended up filming an entire video series that ultimately led to this book. Your insight and expertise in video, editing, and captivating an audience is unsurpassed.

Sandy Lawrence, and your team at Perceptive Marketing. Thank you for your expertise in editing and marketing. I learned so much in this process and appreciate your brilliance, wisdom, and experience. Your insights on this project were invaluable and your excitement and passion for my book inspired me.

Rick Goldberg. Thank you Rick for being one of the people in my life that could see farther down the road than I could. Your vision and support has been a solid rock to stand on since the beginning. In addition to being a visionary who shares wisdom and insight with me, you are a great friend.

CONTENTS

FORWARD

Before I ever met Robert Andrews personally, I knew him well. As a coach of our USA National Gymnastics Team I found myself in numerous conversations with athletes he had worked with and had a significant impact on. The terminology I later learned had originated with Robert and had begun to work its way into the lexicon of the team and many of the coaches; something that couldn't be missed when we would all gather 6 or 7 times a year for training camps. Nothing could be more surprising than to suddenly hear 20-something athletes using terms like "mindfulness" and "accountability" and "ownership" in meaningful ways. The transformation of the culture within the team was subtle, but unmistakable.

Looking at the history of gymnastics performance globally, you can identify 3 distinct development "eras" within the sport. The first was dominated by the initial success of teams that had a cultural basis within their country for participation in the sport. Germany, Czechoslovakia and Finland had made gymnastics a fundamental part of their physical education in schools and even had social clubs throughout their countries that centered around gymnastics activities. This dominated until the Japanese, and later the Soviets, began to focus on optimizing the technical aspects of how the sport is coached.

Finally, the Soviets and Chinese, and to some degree the Romanians, raised the level of conditioning and physical preparation that now defines the modern gymnast.

Today, in high-end sports performance, there is seldom a significant enough difference in physical abilities to account for the difference in competitive performance and results. Part of that gap can be explained through coaching techniques and expertise, but all too often the ultimate difference is only truly explained through understanding mental preparation. This can take many forms, and this book will give you an understanding of these specific areas required by different athletes at different phases of their development. Robert has compiled an artful guide to coaches, athletes and parents on what these areas are, how they impact performance, and how anyone can use them to improve their competitive results. This advice is possibly the most important you will receive in your coaching career. I often hear coaches speak about how mental training is as important as physical training, but I seldom see them commit the same energy to both. A great start would be to study the material here as closely as you do any technical material.

As an example, the information on injury recovery generally available to coaches inevitably includes strengthening, conditioning, range of motion, and weight bearing exercises. In many cases this misses the main point in recovery. If an athlete doesn't completely believe that they are recovered, that it is safe for them to engage in their activities as if the injury never occurred; the chances are very slim that their re-introduction to training will be successful. In 1993 I had an athlete, Jair Lynch, who had competed in the 1992 Olympics in Barcelona. While at the Olympic games he had suffered a sprained ankle, something every athlete in every sport has to deal with at some point. However, in this case the injury lingered and led to a loss in confidence as the pressures inherit in being an Olympic athlete mounted. Following a full year of frustration and failures, I made the difficult decision to shut down his training and build his program back up from scratch. The decision was ultimately the best thing we could have done as Jair went on to win the Silver Medal on Parallel Bars in Atlanta at the 1996 Olympics, but at the time it was the most difficult action I had ever taken with an elite gymnast. Had I known Robert and been exposed to his process for dealing with the complete athlete, including the mental aspects of injury rehabilitation, this entire process would have been done more smoothly, professionally and intelligently. This book will give you the tools to understand and implement this process, something I can only wish I had available as a young coach.

Additionally, while working with the national team together, Robert helped guide me through an incident that threatened my ability to reach and work with a gymnast that ultimately competed on our 2016 Olympic Team. In training, I had made a sarcastic remark that was clearly out of line. I knew it immediately, but my apology to him privately had not seemed to be equal to the damage I felt I had done to our relationship. Robert encouraged me to apologize in our next team meeting, in front of everyone. It was the best advice possible. To this day, that athlete and I have a solid relationship; it made me feel more confident, not less, in addressing the team going forward. Robert's approach to authenticity and ownership had made me a better coach.

In the years since meeting Robert and working side by side with him at dozens of national team camps, I have come to appreciate the value of sports psychology more than I ever had before. I have seen him bring dozens of techniques and tools to bear with athletes and coaches, and had many discussions with him about how this extends to parents. To this day we often speak weekly about issues affecting athletic performance. I have seen his impact on teams and athletes in a dozen other sports, often beginning with seeing athletes on professional teams using his terminology in exactly the same way I had seen with my own team members 10 years ago. I have referred athletes to his practice on many occasions, with the most satisfying of results; athletes overcoming fears, injuries and "plateaus" to go on to higher levels of performance in each case. With this book, you can take advantage of these same "game-changers". The information within is presented in a highly accessible style, with examples and guidelines that make these approaches achievable for you. This is the kind of resource that was simply not widely available in the past. Now, there is no reason to have sports psychology issues be a constraint on your success.

Dave Juszczyk USA Olympic and National Team Gymnastics Coach

TESTIMONIALS FOR CHAMPION'S MENTAL EDGE

"Mr. Andrews has helped me realize my potential by getting me to center my focus when I'm ready to compete, or anytime mindfulness is needed. With his guidance, my confidence in my abilities and myself were restored. His assistance was instrumental in my reaching my goal of becoming an Olympic and World Champion."

Simone Biles Olympic and World Champion

"Robert helped me visualize positive outcomes at major competitions before I even stepped foot on a competition floor. His professional wisdom and words have highly impacted my success today as a business owner and family man.

Sean Townsend Olympian and World Champion

'Robert's work is transformational! His performance model is the link between peak performance and self-mastery. He helped me dive deep and emerge with a new set of beliefs that led to my best years as an athlete. I am now an Olympic Medalist and owe so much of my success to Robert.

Raj Bhavsar Olympic Medalist

"Robert has helped me achieve and maintain my peak performance level for many years, going back to my college days. I will continue to count on him as I strive to perfect my craft as an NFL Quarterback."

Case Keenum Professional Football Player

"Robert has worked with several of my elite gymnasts. I am certain his influence has helped my girls succeed at the national, international & Olympic levels. Robert has played a critical role in helping me develop successful world class gymnasts"

Maggie Haney U.S.A. National, World, and Olympic gymnastics coach

I began working with Robert Andrews after an injury kept me out of competition in 2009. As an Olympian who had sought out sport psychologists consistently throughout my career, the mental aspect of training was not a new idea to me. The work that Robert did with me was so practical and applicable to my day-to-day training; I wish that we had begun our work together years earlier. Now, as a coach, I am able to apply the concepts Robert taught me as I work with young athletes. Because of the impact Robert had on my career, I am excited that this book will make his concepts and approach available to everyone.

Erica Fraley Olympic Pole Vaulter

INTRODUCTION

Athletes, want to have more confidence and more belief in yourself?

Are you an athlete struggling to meet your full potential? Do you need to learn how to master your mind and emotions to be your best at critical times of competition? Maybe you just can't get over that time you struck out in the big game, fell on the ice, missed a game winning field goal, or had the gymnastics meet won and fell on your last event.

Maybe you are an athlete who is already performing at a high level and you want to gain a serious advantage over your competition.

Welcome to the Champion's Mental Edge™ for athletes, coaches, teams and parents. I've spent most of my life developing this performance model from my own experiences and my experiences working with athletes of all levels. Now I want to share this same powerful information with you. I am confident that it will change your life in and out of sports.

In this performance program, we will start off by doing an athlete's assessment that looks at key indicators of performance.

- What's going on for you on a mental, emotional and physical level when you are at your best?

- What's happening to you and what happens to your performance when you're struggling?

- What are your warning signs that indicate you're heading for trouble?

- How does pressure and stress impact your performance and change your performance temperament and personality?

Then, we're going to look at how you utilize your mental and emotional energy--the resources so vital for peak performance. How do stress and distractions push in on you and change things for you, the athlete?

Parents will have access to needed information on how to be a better ally and resource to help their athlete maximize performance. There's also information in this book for coaches, on how to define the common traits of championship cultures.

When you pull the information from this model together and integrate what you learn into training and ultimately into competition, you will have more confidence, more belief in yourself and a stronger ability to stay mentally and emotionally centered and balanced, no matter what the game brings your way. The information in *Champion's Mental Edge©* *for Athletes* will help you have more passion during training and competition. More importantly, you have fun competing in the sport that you love.

I was a 3-Sport athlete in high school. I tried to play in college, but the mental game got the best of me. I suffered serious injuries, and realized I didn't know how to handle the pressure and stress that came with competing at that high level. With that and other life experiences, I began my amazing journey in the world of sports. Who would have thought, in the future, I would end up working with athletes competing in numerous Olympic games, beginning with the 2008 Beijing Olympics. I've worked with Olympic gold, silver, and bronze medalists, world Champion's in many sports, NBA All Stars, NFL All Pros, Major League Baseball

All Stars and Heisman Trophy winners.

This book isn't meant for just elite athletes. It will help you whether you are an athlete in junior high or high school, a college athlete, a weekend tri-athlete, a weekend warrior, own your own business or you are the CEO of a corporation. The performance information in this book will change your game.

Let's get started.

THE ATHLETE'S PERFORMANCE ASSESSMENT

"Since we can't change reality, let us change the eyes which see reality" Nikos Kazantzakis

Let's start with the Athlete's Assessment. In this exercise, you will learn a lot about yourself in and away from your sport. You will increase awareness about who you are as an athlete and as a person. You will assess where you are now in relation to your potential talent, where you want to go in your sport, and how to identify and understand what gets in the way of you being your best.

We will also look at what keeps you from consistently performing at your best. I do an assessment with every athlete I work with during our first session together. This is how you get started. This assessment is where you're going to discover awareness to what makes you tick and what happens when things go wrong on the court, on the field or in the pool.

Get a piece of paper, a pen, and be honest with yourself. Nobody's going to read this but you, unless you want to share it. The more honest you can be with yourself, the farther you can go with this process. Don't hold anything back. Go for it. Be honest. Get your pen. Get your paper. Let's start.

When you are at your absolute best

First, describe yourself when you are at your absolute best, when you are in the zone, when things are flowing on the court. The basket looks huge; you're jumping higher than you've ever jumped; you're unstoppable; you're filled with passion.

What I usually hear, when talking one-on-one with athletes is this, "I'm passionate. I'm focused. I'm confident. I'm plugged in. I'm smiling. I'm having a good time. Nobody can stop me."

We are looking at what it's like when you compete at your absolute best. We are not just talking about your physical attributes. We're not talking about how fast you run, how flexible you feel, or how quick or explosive you are. The physical aspect is only a part of it. Your physical performance is just part of the equation. If you notice, a lot of what I talk about has to do with behavior. It also has a lot to do with personality, emotion and passion. Those are the fuel for your body, your talent, and potential.

Next, think back to a time when you really delivered. Maybe, it was at a state championship gymnastics meet, or a regional track meet. Maybe it was when there were runners on base, two outs, bottom of the last inning of the game, and you got up to hit and *YOU* delivered. You knew you were going to hit the ball. You hit that double in the gap and brought in the winning runs. I want to know that athlete. I want to know "Who is that athlete"? Spend time writing down your responses because when you are done we are going to flip your perspective.

Now, get up. Move to another place in the room. Sit in a different chair in your living room or breakfast room. If you are in your bedroom, move to a different room. I want you to experience a shift in your mind and making a physical shift will result in a cognitive shift. I want to change your mind and your perspective about the way you think, through this next exercise.

When you are really struggling

Describe how you feel when you are really struggling, when it's just dreadful. It's awful. You're getting beat. You can't get to the backcourt fast enough. You drop passes. You are falling. You are over rotating your dismount on the floor, falling on the beam, running through on pole vault, or whatever the situation might be for you. During the last 50 meters of that 200-meter butterfly, it felt like there was a gorilla on your back and you felt heavy in the water.

I want to know about when you were sluggish, not having fun. Your passion diminished and confidence was low. You were thinking too much, worried about what other people were thinking and worried about the college scouts in the stands watching you in the volleyball match.

I want to know about that time you felt heavy and your thoughts were negative. I worked with a kid once who said, "I start thinking too many don't thoughts. You know, don't walk this batter! Don't pop out! Don't strike out!"

I asked you to move to a different chair because I want you to split these two athletes in your mind. Both have the same talent. Assuming you are healthy, it's the same talent. Nothing changed about your talent. You have the same height, weight, core strength, flexibility, power, endurance, explosiveness and quickness. That talent is innate, and yet we have two different athletes, living in the same body. I want you to capture that difference. I want you to separate these different athletes in your mind. Inside you there is this great, glorious, magnificent athlete, and then, you've got the struggling athlete. For some athletes the change takes place quickly, say after a bad play. For others the change takes place over time. Constant belittling from a coach, issues with a teammate, or a poor mindset can cause this transformation to take days or weeks to occur.

What are your warning signs?

I want you to think about and write down, "What are the warning signs that things are starting to change?"

Imagine, you and I are having lunch together outside and a storm starts building. Nature gives us very clear signs that the storm is coming. Clouds begin to build up; wind picks up; temperatures drop; the trees start to blow. We might see lightning in the distance or hear thunder, and then we hear and smell the rain. All these are very clear signs that a storm is coming. Every athlete has similar warnings.

What are your warning signs that performance is beginning to decline? I have worked with athletes who start overthinking, get angry and frustrated, shut down and get quiet, withdraw, get butterflies in their stomach, or get tightness in their chest.

What are warnings signs that things are heading south for you? They might be very subtle. I worked with a gymnast once who told me she would mess with her eyebrows. Another girl stuck her tongue out of the left side of her mouth, but she didn't realize that was her warning sign. I've even had athletes bite their jersey.

I worked with a college soccer player who would start yelling at her teammates when she got stressed. Yelling was one of the warning signs that she was starting to lose it. The team came up with a code word for her that meant, "Hey, you are starting to lose it. You are starting to get off center." The code word helped bring her back into balance mentally and emotionally.

You must know your triggers, your warning signs. They can be obvious. For example, you blow up, get angry, and yell at people, or you shut down. Warning signals can be very subtle. You may bite your nails, or play with your hands before a volleyball serve.

On your worksheet, write down your warning signs. Those signs tell you that things are starting to change with your thinking, with your attitude about the game, and with your perception. Pressure is building and your performance will begin to change. Your physical talent is not changing. It's the way you approach the game, and the way you approach the game is in direct response to your specific warning signs. As things begin to build, triggers start to set you off.

What are your triggers?

Finally, let's identify those things that get to you. What are the triggers? What pushes your buttons? What sets you off? Is it a bad call in a game? Did you think you just did the best gymnastic routine of your life, but you got a horribly low score? Perhaps it was a coach's comment, a parent rolling their eyes in the stands, or an opposing player trying to get in your head. Recognize what pushes your buttons, such as missing a shot, missing a layup, or making a mistake. Recognizing your triggers prepares you to head into the concept I call 'mindfulness.' It is a very powerful concept for athletes, so let's dive into this concept a little deeper!

MINDFULNESS AND SELF-AWARENESS IN SPORTS

"You have to be able to center yourself, to let all of your emotions go. Don't ever forget that you play with your soul as well as your body"
Kareem Abdul Jabbar

Mindfulness is one of the most powerful concepts when it comes to improving sports performance. I was interviewed by an organization that was interested in the work I do. They asked me, "Of all of the things that you teach athletes, what do you think is the most significant, the most powerful tool?"

Without hesitation I answered, "Mindfulness."

They asked, "What is mindfulness to you?"

I told them *"Mindfulness is an awareness of what you're doing when you are doing it."*

One of them said, "That's really remarkable." Then he pulled out a book and handed it to me. The book was written by Viktor Frankl, an artist, sculptor and painter. Frankl went through some horrible traumas in his life. He lost his wife and daughter during the Holocaust. He learned to calm his horrible traumas by being remarkably mindful in how he approached his life. He wrote, *"Between stimulus and response there's a small space of time and in that space of time lies our ability to make choices. Those choices decide our growth and our happiness."*

I said, "That is the perfect definition of mindfulness. That's it!" We had an amazing conversation about mindfulness and expanded on this concept. I could tell they "got it."

I hope you'll get it too because this can be a game changer for you. In the Athlete's Assessment I teach you to recognize your warning signs and the need to become more mindful, more aware. It's like putting a little version of you on your shoulder who whispers just to you, "Hey, you're doing great,"

"Your mindset is great," "You've got this!" When you are struggling, that little voice might whisper, "Uh, oh, you're starting to be a little frustrated," "You're starting to get angry.

Your breathing patterns are changing. You are rushing things. You're walking down the golf course too fast."

Stimulus + Response = Outcome

That's all mindfulness is--that inner voice that identifies when things are working and when things are starting to get off a bit. I took Viktor Frankl's quote and broke it down into a formula: **Stimulus + Response = Outcome**. The stimulus is what happens. The referee called a foul on you and there's no way you even touched the other player. Did your gymnastics routine get a bad score even though you thought you nailed it? What about the coach's booming voice while you're concentrating on striking out the batter? Your teammate dropped a baton when you're in the third leg of the sprint relay at the state meet.

Events happen, stimulus happens. The key is your response to the stimulus. What matters most is how you respond and whether or not you have *mindfulness* about how to respond in the right way. That's one of the more powerful things about sports. Sports can expose your weaknesses. Mindfulness can help strengthen your weaknesses. Mindfulness helps you overcome adversity. It can help you learn how to recognize and make choices about how you respond to stressors related to performance. The event could be, somebody makes a hard foul on a layup. You get to decide how you want to respond. You can go right back at them and get a stupid foul, or you can take a few deep breaths, hit both free throws and shut them down on defense. It's your choice. You can mindfully respond in the moment or react in ways that are destructive to performance.

Your reaction is not about your coach, your parents, the scouts in the stands or your opponent. Your reaction is about you. You get to decide how you want to respond. Some in the world of sports performance like to use the word "event" because some say stimulus sounds a little too technical. S+R=O or, Event + Response = Outcome, E+R=O. It's the same formula. My experience working with athletes shows many don't have a clue about what, why, or how they're responding to stimuli during competition. I compare these athletes to the ball in the pinball machine. They are at the mercy of the game. They bounce all over the place and don't have the self-awareness or tools to get back in that zone, to get back to their center, or to recognize when they're starting to have a meltdown.

Many athletes develop a default reaction and get angry, frustrated, get quiet or completely shut down. They hunch their shoulders over, walk too fast or rush. They have no awareness of what is happening.

In later sections, we will look at the way athletes waste

valuable energy by not being mindful or aware of their reactivity. There is a simple exercise I want you to do. I give every athlete a wristband that reads, 'Mind of a Champion.' I want you to find one of those rubber wristbands somewhere.

You can order them online. You can find them at your favorite sporting goods store. I want you to get one and make a commitment to yourself to wear it for 21 days. You can wear it longer if you want. Athletes from all over the country email me, "Hey can you mail me some more wristbands."

They tell me stories like, "Mine broke when the trainers cut my tape off after practice." A swimmer puts her band on top of her bag before she swims, and it disappears because somebody wants a piece of the action. Someone took the wristband, so I sent her another one.

Find a wristband and commit to wear it for 21 days. Here's how it works. Anytime you think a negative thought that is limiting, produces doubt, erodes your self-confidence, increases stress, pressure, fear, or anxiety; you take the wristband off and move it to the other wrist. You correct the negative thought into a positive one. Example, change the thought "I'll never be able to hit this pitcher" to "I'm working hard on catching up to his fast ball." Change "I hate beam" to "Beam is something I'm getting better at." Or, "I'm working hard to improve my scores."

I once worked with an Olympic gymnast who said, "High

Bar is my worst event."

I told him, "I never want to hear you say that again."

He asked, "Why?"

I said, "Because as long as you think that thought, High Bar will be your worst event." He changed his thinking to, "High Bar is the event I'm working on the hardest."

Here's another way to help you with this. Do you use a GPS system on your car or your phone? You have to play a game 25 miles away and you think you know how to get there but you're not sure, so you enter the address into your phone or your GPS. Then the lady with the nice voice starts telling you go seven miles on Interstate 87, take a left and such and such. What happens when you make a wrong turn? You get re-routed, right? That re-routing puts you back on track.

That's what this wristband exercise does for you. It re-routes you. It's a GPS system that helps you get back on track when you start getting off balance, either with your emotional reaction to events, or your mental reactions to stimuli or your body language, the way your body responds. It's a powerful mindfulness tool to use so you can GPS yourself back on track repeatedly.

I've worked with athletes who try this for a day or two and tell me, "It really didn't work." It takes commitment to make it work. If you're learning a new skill such as a new move in cheerleading, or how to throw a new pitch, or a different kind of defensive coverage for a defensive back, you don't get it the first time. It takes time. What I'm teaching you requires hard work, dedication, and commitment.

I work with a fencer on the U. S. National Team, who really struggled to grasp these concepts. After a lot of work, he told me, "I've gotten so good at it that I know what my body is supposed to feel like when I step on the strip. I don't have to think about breathing. I don't have to think about being mindful. I don't have to think about correcting my thoughts. It has become automatic. It's just part of my game now. It's just how I do things."

I worked with another athlete who competed in track. His team was in Houston for a big track meet and they were running that evening. He found me on the Internet and came to see me before the meet. We figured out that he had no awareness about the concept of mindfulness. He was running with way too much intensity. He was the athlete you saw take off way ahead of the pack, blowing everybody away, but then he ran out of energy. Most of the other runners passed him and he came in near the back of the pack. He had no awareness about how much energy he was spending or why he was starting so fast. This athlete left my office at 10:30 in the morning. By the time he ran at 5:30 that afternoon, he changed his wristband 42 times. He called me after the race and said, "I won the race by 15 meters and I ran my fastest time ever by nine seconds." He was ecstatic and said, "It was my mindset that was causing me to start out too fast, to go out with too much adrenaline. My negative thinking created so much anxiety it caused me to run out of energy at the end of the race."

I hope you understand the power that mindfulness and self-awareness play in performance. This is the most significant tool I can teach you. Get your wristband. Go to work. Change your game.

ATHLETE'S PEAK PERFORMANCE ZONE

This segment is about another important performance concept, your *Peak Performance Zone.* If you have ever experienced a performance where everything felt just right, things felt simple and easy, and you performed at extraordinary levels, then you have been in "your zone." The zone is that place where you have the right amount of adrenaline, neurological stimulation, and intensity. When you described yourself at your best in the Athlete's Assessment, you were describing yourself in your peak performance zone.

When you're in the *Peak Performance Zone,* great things are happening. In our assessment section, we talked about you at your best. All those traits, qualities, and attributes are the contributing factors that lead to you performing at your best. You've probably heard athletes say, "I was just in the zone. I was really feeling it that night."

Think about what being in the zone means. The zone exists in every athlete. I'd like you to get a piece of paper and pen and make a big L on your page. Along the bottom on the left write 0. On the bottom right, write 10. At the top of the "L" write 10. Under the bottom of the L write "Pressure" and on the top write "Performance." I'm going to show you that there is a very strong connection between the level of intensity, pressure, adrenaline, neurological stimulation and your level of performance.

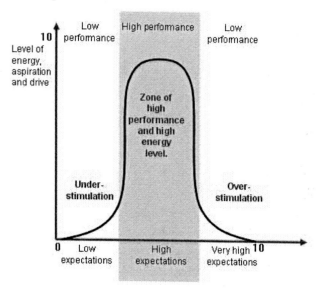

Achieving the highest level of performance, you can imagine.

The right amount of pressure and intensity produces the highest level of performance. The secret is to know how to get into YOUR zone. Earlier you wrote that you perform at your best when everything is running on all cylinders. You have the right amount of intensity and the right amount of pressure. You begin to move out of your zone when those warning signs, I asked you to talk about, start kicking in. You start biting your nails, get butterflies in your stomach, start getting irritable, shut down or have poor body language. Those signs are your mind and your body's way of telling you that stress and pressure are beginning to increase. If you don't listen to the warning signs, your pressure is either going to move too high or too low and affect performance in a negative way. Go back to the concepts we discussed in the athlete's assessment. We identified the different athletes that exist in you. We worked on mindfulness, taught the wristband technique, installed your internal GPS system, and looked at your warning signs. Now you can understand this concept around pressure and its impact on performance.

Why does pressure change?

Pressure changes with changes in thought, attitude and perception. How do athletes change their thoughts? How do they change their perception? How do they change their attitude about their performance? Your coach says to you, "That was a great job last night." You feel good about yourself. It has a calming effect on your mind. Your parents get in the car after you've hit the winning home run and they love you up. This affirmation has an effect that is soothing to you. It is empowering.

The opposite of that is also true. You struck out with bases loaded in the last inning. You get in the car and your parents turn to you in the backseat and say, "Why did you strike out in that last at bat?" Sadly, I hear such stories often. These types of comments change your perception about yourself. They can change your attitude about your performance. Maybe it changes your attitude about your parents.

I talked earlier about what happens if you don't get the right score in a great gymnastics routine. Perhaps you double faulted during a key point of a tennis match. That can change your thoughts, attitude and perception, which can cause internal pressure to increase. It literally changes the kind of hormones that are being produced in your brain and in your body.

Graph your ideal levels of combined intensity, stress,

pressure, and adrenaline. Perhaps you start beating yourself up, getting angry, irritable, or shutting down. Your pressure is going to change. If your chart score moves up to an eight or nine and you don't listen to the warning signs, the eight, nine, or ten level of pressure is going to impact performance profoundly.

You may be the kind of athlete who shuts down, or the kind of athlete who turns on yourself, or your intensity levels drop. I worked with a number of baseball and softball pitchers who have three different athletes inside of them.

These pitchers have one pitcher who is in the zone. I'm hearing numbers like five, six or seven. Let's say they're at five. When they're pitching at a five, they're moving the ball in and out, they're hitting their spots, and they're changing speeds. They're confident. They have an edge over that hitter before the hitter ever steps into the box. They are in their zone.

The shortstop makes a couple errors. The pitcher starts getting irritable. They start rushing their mechanics. They start trying to overthrow and pressure kicks up to an eight or nine. They're changing the way they approach the game and as a result they're going to struggle.

The second baseman misses a pop up. The first baseman missed an easy ground ball. The pitcher reacts in a way that lowers pressure. Their pressure level drops to a two or three.

There is not enough intensity, not enough adrenaline, and not enough stimulation. That's going to result in a completely different pitcher. One that is more apathetic, maybe not as focused, or maybe too worried about what people are thinking. We see there can be three different athletes. That can be true for a hockey goalie, a basketball player, a guy ready to kick a field goal to win a football game or a player in the NFL playoff game. You want to have that best athlete present consistently.

Stay in your zone

That's why it is so important to be in your zone before you execute that kick, shoot those critical free throws, or get ready to make an attempt at a national qualifying jump. You want to make the national team? Do you want to be at an eight, nine or ten, or a three or four? Or do you want to be in your peak performance zone? Learning how to recognize your warning signs is critical. Learning how to recognize the way things are changing in your body, and learning how to bring yourself back into balance mentally and emotionally, is the key to staying in your zone.

When you stay in your zone, your performance is not only going to improve, but will continue to improve on a very consistent level. That's when you get the athlete rising to the occasion. You hear about the mentally tough athlete. Nothing gets to them because they know how to stay in their zone. Nothing knocks them off center. Nothing knocks them off balance. They have learned how to recognize the triggers that set them off and how to get back into that place of power and total engagement.

When you're in the zone, you're in the place of power. That's when great things happen. Work with that. You can integrate this into your life. Suppose you're a high school or college student and you're walking across campus on your way to class. You're at a three or four, just hanging out with your friends and having a good day. You walk into class and the professor says, "We have a pop quiz today."

"Oh, my God, I'm at a nine." You start taking the test and think, "Uh, wow I read the right material last night. I got this. I'm back down to a four again." Suppose you're eating lunch with friends and you're at a two. You're on the way to practice. You're late and you're back up to an eight. Watch yourself for a few days and see how that number moves in response to the things that happen in your day.

In an earlier section, we covered S + R = O. Your response is going to increase pressure, decrease pressure or keep pressure where it needs to be. For example, you give up a bomb to the first batter of the game--that's the event, that's the stimulus, and then you decide how to respond. The way you respond is going to increase or decrease that pressure and that's where *mindfulness* comes in. This is where you use your wristband and work with breathing techniques that we will talk about later. The key is staying in your zone.

I have an absolutely remarkable story that took place at the Beijing Olympics. I had worked with Raj Bhavsar, a member of the U.S. Olympic gymnastics team for a year prior to the Olympics. The U.S. team wasn't expected to even make it to the team finals, but they did. Nobody expected them to be there, much less win a medal. Raj had to perform at a very high level under tremendous pressure on his last event to secure a bronze medal for the team. He was waiting to start his routine and started thinking about the 20,000 people in the arena and the hundreds of millions of people around the world watching. I had dinner with Raj after the Olympics. I asked if there was anything we worked on that helped prepare for that moment.

He told me, "I was thinking about all those crazy things and I checked in with myself. On a scale from 0-10, I was at a 12. I knew that if I started pommel horse at a 12, I would fall. So I stopped. I became *mindful.* I focused my thoughts on the people who had helped me get there. I saw an Olympic official putting a medal around my neck.

Raj's peak performance zone was 7, so he worked with mindfulness and with breathing to get his level down as close to a 7 as possible. He knew the intensity would not go away. After all, this was the Olympic games. He got it as close to a 7 as he could. He saluted the judges and started his routine. He nailed it. I have a picture in my waiting room of Raj with an Olympic medal around his neck. He said if he had tried that routine at a 12, the Olympics would be a different story. He wouldn't be an Olympic medalist.

This technique works and it works at the highest level. Go ahead and put it to work now. Now that we've looked at understanding your Peak Performance Zone, let's move on to another very important topic--helping you understand how to maximize your physical, mental and emotional energy as an athlete.

MAXIMIZING YOUR MENTAL AND
EMOTIONAL RESOURCES

"I am building a fire, and every day I train, I add more fuel. At just
the right moment, I light the match"

Mia Hamm

In this section I am going to cover what I consider to be another pillar of peak performance--Energy Management. To define it even more clearly, this section is about gaining recognition and clarity about what you do with your mental, emotional and physical resources for performance.

Many athletes spend too much energy focusing on the

physical aspects of performance: getting stronger, more mobile, more powerful, quicker, more explosive, and other physical attributes. Physical development is certainly vital to athletic performance. There is another area that I want to explore with you that can help you maximize your physical talent and potential.

A few years ago, I worked with an athlete who was a big, strong, talented baseball pitcher. He was not meeting his full potential. He was going out and getting lit up and only lasting for part of an inning before he was taken out of the game. He remembered his coach coming out and taking the ball, and him walking off the field with his head down. I am not talking about just one pitcher. I worked with many baseball and softball pitchers who have had similar experiences.

In our first session together this athlete said, "When I throw a pitch I don't know where the ball is going to go. I feel like my hand is all over the place."

As his mental training expert, I told him, "If your hand is all over the place, that means your mind is all over the place." I saw the light bulb go off in this guy's head.

I asked, "What was that? What does that response mean?"

He told me, "That makes a lot of sense."

I asked, "Which part?"

He said, "I've been so embarrassed about the way I'm pitching that I haven't called my parents or returned their calls for two weeks. I got into an argument with my girlfriend over a stupid disagreement. I have too much pride, so I haven't talked to her in three days. I'm way behind in my schoolwork. I have unpaid parking tickets with the university. I even have unpaid tickets with the city. I have two nails in my tires and I have to stop all the time to put air in my tires."

I listened to him and then said, "Write all those down." He wrote them down and I said, "Now, I want you to go through this list, and I want you to assign an energetic value to each item on the list." A zero means that item takes up none of your brainpower; none of your mental and emotional energy, and 100 means it's taking up a lot of energy.

He assigned values to each thing on his list and each one had a very high, what I call, stress value. He made a commitment to start scratching things off his list, which meant he tied up loose ends and took care of business. He called his parents and apologized and explained he hadn't been returning their calls because he was just too embarrassed. He called his girlfriend and took her out to dinner, apologized, said he was being stubborn and made up with her. He stayed up four or five nights in a row taking care of his schoolwork. He paid off all his tickets with the city and paid off his tickets with the university. Then he went to the tire store and got a new tire because he had waited too long to repair the old one. He took care of everything on his stress list just like he took an eraser and erased all of them out of his brain.

I asked him, "How do you feel now?"

He said, "I feel like I just took a bunch of rocks out of my backpack. I feel so much lighter. My mind is so much clearer and sharper." This guy went from being an 88-90 mph pitcher to a 92-93 mph guy. He was staying in games four, five and six innings, striking out hitters, keeping hitters off balance, contributing to his team and ending his career on a very high note.

I worked with Olympic pole-vaulter Erica Bartolina, now Erica Fraley. When I started working with her, I went online and found a picture of her on the runway. She looked so tense. You could see the tightness in the tendons through her neck and shoulders. She looked ripped, but something didn't look right. I found a picture of the Russian world record holder at the exact same place on the runway holding the pole in the exact same position, and she looked relaxed. The Russian athlete also looked very athletic, but she looked much more relaxed than Erica.

I showed Erica the two pictures and she told me, "I have to make sure and get everything right. Everything has to be in the right place for me to jump high!"

I suggested, "Let's approach this in a different way. Sometimes less is more!" We looked at ways she was wasting energy in her approach to vaulting, especially her approach as she came down the runway. It took about six months before she bought into the idea of competing with more passion and more enjoyment. She had to let go of control and rigidness. She had to let go of perfectionism. As she let go, she could be more relaxed in her approach and through the jump. A few months after we started working together she went to Europe for a big competition. She sent me a photo of her clearing her highest height ever by 6 to 8 inches. She said it was so easy to go higher that it scared her at first, that it would take time to get comfortable with this new approach.

My final story is about a gymnast I worked with who was trying to make the US Olympic team. She was working on the beam. These little "mom and me" gymnasts would come by the beam and distract her. She came to me because she was so frustrated. "I'm trying to get this new beam routine down and these kids walk by and they're such a distraction. I get so angry and frustrated with them."

I said, "You're missing a huge opportunity to integrate some mental training tools and concepts here."

She said, "What do you mean?"

I said, "If you can't handle little "mom and me" gymnasts, how do you expect to handle NBC cameras right over the beam looking at your every move and those same cameras focusing on you after an event."

She sighed, "Man, that's a good point. I didn't think about it that way." So, she quit wasting that energy and she used those kids as a way to learn how to stay focused and locked in. As a result, she got better on beam.

What do all three of these stories have in common? They are all about athletes who are wasting vital resources and letting energy leak away. Once this critical energy is gone, they don't get it back.

So, the secret to success is learning how to really take an honest look at your life and make an assessment in key areas and figure out where you are wasting mental and emotional energy. Find out where you're giving away power you need for performance.

In my work with athletes, I have identified four key areas where athletes tend to waste a lot of energy. We will take a detailed look at each one.

Category One: Procrastination

I want you to get a pen and paper again. Be completely honest with yourself. Where in your life do you procrastinate or put things off? We all do this. I meet very few athletes who aren't procrastinators on some level.

It could be schoolwork, chores around the house, or part of your training regimen. Maybe it is getting something fixed that's important to you, which you really need, and you put it off until it creates stress in your brain. We're talking about brainpower. When you procrastinate you let distractions take up space in your mental computer. You want all that energy going into performance. If energy is leaking off into the areas that you're procrastinating, the energy doesn't go into training and ultimately it doesn't show up in your performance. So, take an honest look in that area.

Category Two: People, Situations or Actions That You Tolerate

I've had athletes who have been in bad relationships with someone who was needy or clingy or just not what I call "a battery." They don't buy into your vision of yourself as an athlete. I'm not saying it must be all about you or you must be selfish. But if you want to be successful, you must have relationships in your life that feed you rather than drain you. I see so many athletes who tolerate bad or even toxic relationships with people that they allow to drain a lot of energy from them. It's as if they plug cables into them and allow them to drain energy. Sometimes you should do what I call pulling weeds. You're trying to grow this fabulous garden, so you've got to pull the weeds out. The weeds are the people sucking the life out of you. Negative relationships pull on you.

Those relationships might come from people in your organization, parents, coaches or teammates. You might have some work to do here. I believe that we teach people how to treat us by what we allow, what we stop and what we reinforce. If you're tolerating things that are not feeding your training or your performance, you're losing energy.

You might tolerate bad training equipment, a negative coach or teammate, your own poor attitude or an injury that you won't get looked at. These "tolerations" add up and rob you of energy vital to your performance.

Category Three: Areas in Your Life Where You Are Distracted.

Do you allow your mind to wander? Where do you waste energy by being preoccupied by things that don't feed performance?

I've worked with athletes who constantly compare themselves to other athletes. The other athlete's physique, or how they warm up, or even their presence can intimidate them. They allow their mind to start buying into, "They're better than me." You're comparing yourself to them constantly.

You could be distracted by not completing assignments or

showing up late for team meetings. Distractions are another area where you've got to take an honest look.

Where Are You Totally Stressed out?

You could have had a bad automobile accident, so you must work with insurance companies. Maybe you're distracted about how you're going to get a new car and you've got to get to tryouts.

I had a coach once who was being tough on his athletes. I was doing a coaching workshop at his school. During a break he said, "I just want to thank you. You've opened my eyes to something. I know I've been tough on my athletes these last few weeks and now I know why. My wife and two young kids are at home. It's August and our air-conditioning is out. I don't have the money to fix the air-conditioner. I'm scared and I'm frustrated. I'm a little bit ashamed that I'm not earning enough income to fix it. My kids and wife are at home suffering and I've been taking it out on my athletes." He was stressed out.

Stressors on your list might be serious. If they're serious, ask for help. You can get help from school counselors or other people on campus that might help you. If there are things that you can't handle, then seek help.

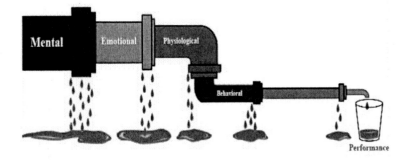

Performance

Stress Score

I want you to go through your list and put a check mark on all the things that you can do something about. Check off items where you can take ownership and responsibility. Check those things, and then get to work scratching them off your list.

Look at each item in each of the four stress categories you wrote about. Rank each item from 0 to 100. Zero means the area is not taking up any of your brainpower and none of your mental and emotional energy. One hundred means that the stressor is taking up as much energy as you can imagine. These numbers don't have to add up to 100. You might have five 100s, a 65, a 40, and so on. Give each stressor a value and trust your intuition. You might decide, "Man, this is a big one, it's 85. This next one, not cleaning my room when my parents tell me, that's a 65. I've got this huge project due Monday, and I've got a three-day baseball tournament this weekend, so I haven't even started the project. That's a 90."

Assign a number to each of those items on your list. When you're done, total it up and that's going to be your total stress score. Do this for each of the four categories we covered. When you go into competition, I want your stress scores to be as low as possible. It's alarming to me that I see athletes with stress scores of 900, 1000, as high as 1440. And they wonder why they can't do backward tumbling, throw strikes, or why they're getting beat on defensive coverage. They're not running as fast as they can, because so much of their brainpower isn't focused on performance. It's not focused on letting their body do what it can do. Their brains are focused on all those stressors that are going on around them. They are allowing their energy to be drained by things that don't serve peak performance. They are wasting mental and emotional energy and brainpower.

I live in Texas and we have hurricanes come through on a regular basis. After a hurricane you see power lines just flapping around, shooting off sparks. That's what's going on with you. You have all these cables hanging out of you, shooting off energy that's not going into training and not going into performance.

Take this seriously! Make yourself a stress list. Evaluate your stress scores. Identify things you can control and start acting to get these stressors off your list. Ask for help with things you can't manage yourself. See if you can minimize the energy impact these stressors have on you. You're going to find when you reclaim your energy and channel it back into your brain and your body, your performance will shoot through the roof. In our next section, we are addressing the importance of personality and performance. Now go get busy taking care of the stress in your life.

THE IMPORTANCE OF PERSONALITY AND PERFORMANCE

"Only to the extent that we expose ourselves over and over to annihilation, can that which is indestructible be found in us."

Pema Chodron

In this section we are going to look at the power of personality and performance. You might ask, "What does he mean by that?" When a sports magazine once interviewed me, the interviewer asked, "What is your secret to helping athletes prepare for a big event like the Olympic games?"

I said, "It's really simple: Helping them show up

authentically."

The interviewer asked, "What do you mean by that?"

I replied, "I can teach athletes how to breathe and manage stress or distractions, and get into their peak performance zones."

That's all great and necessary, but the real secret is helping the athlete show up with their own unique dynamic, authentic personality, and then pairing their authentic personality with their athletic talent. That's when I see great athletes become Champion's. It's a remarkable process.

To expand on that, I'm going to tell you a story about me that happened many years ago; it seems like a lifetime ago. At that time, I lived in a two-story apartment, and I had been out with some friends the night before. The next morning, I walked out of my bedroom to the balcony, and I looked down and saw the same friends that I'd been out with the night before. They looked up and said, "Hey Robert."

In that moment, I had a sudden flash that was one of those defining, formative moments in my life. I had this flash of insight, this awareness that I am one person with the people I went out with last night. I'm another person with the people I grew up with, and I'm another person at the gym where I work out. I'm yet another person at work. Which one of these people is the real me?

I realized then, when I was young, that I was like a

chameleon. I adapted to whatever situation or environment, and whomever I was with at the time. At that point, I made a decision to start showing up congruently and authentically wherever I went.

What does that have to do with sports? It has everything to do with sports. Athletes, as we've talked about in previous sections, are under constant states of change, stress, pressure, stimulus, and events. I could go all the way down the list of the things that we have already covered. If an athlete doesn't know how to maintain their own integrity and stay true to who they are, they will be that chameleon that changes in the presence of one coach and, then acts another way with a different coach. When scouts are in the room or on the court, they act another way. They're like a tree that is blowing in the wind. There's just not much there. They don't have their roots firmly planted in the ground.

Learning how to recognize yourself at your best, your authentic traits, and the conditioning that causes you to move away from your authentic self, is huge. It is what I consider to be one of the secrets to success and happiness in life.

When I started working with Simone Biles, she was very talented, but was not reaching anywhere near her full potential. She was very quiet and reserved with me. She has told the following story many times publicly, so I will tell it here. One day I asked her why she was so quiet with me?

She said, "I don't want you to think that I'm crazy"

She said she was told this by another athlete, "Only crazy people go see someone like Robert."

I went on to tell her many ways I could help her become the best she could be. She listened and understood that she wasn't crazy. She was very smart to address the mental and emotional aspects of gymnastics. She realized in many ways it could give her an advantage over her competition.

Simone was making a lot of mistakes and errors in competition. I told her, "You know we've got to get you to take your foot off the gas. There's just too much energy going into your performance and you don't look like you're having very much fun."

I said, "Something tells me there's a dynamic personality in there that we need to access and when you weave that dynamic personality into your training, and ultimately your competition, some really remarkable things are going to happen."

Simone got on board and is now one of the greatest athletes in the world. When she competes, not only does the crowd smile, the judges and other competitors are on the edge of their seats watching. It's not just the talent; it's the personality she exhibits when she performs. Her authentic personality is like a magnet. It draws us in and electrifies us. I don't think Simone would have won four Olympic Gold

Medals, and ten World championship Gold Medals, if she had not made the commitment to be Simone on the gymnastics floor. Another critical factor is that Simone had a coach, Aimee Boorman who understood this concept and insisted that Simone be Simone in every aspect of her training and performance.

I once worked with a major league baseball player. When this athlete first came to see me, he was hitting .240. He was struggling and not enjoying the game. When he first came into the league he was filled with wonder and thinking, "Wow, look at these stadiums. I get to dress where Mickey Mantle got dressed, and I'm standing where Reggie Jackson hit his game-winning home-run." This guy loved signing autographs. He was in love with his passion of the game.

And then everybody started having him look at scouting reports, videos, tweaking his swing, correcting something else and keeping up with stats and on-base percentages. He developed a get-it-right mentality. He became afraid of messing up and making mistakes.

These interventions took an athlete filled with love and passion for the game and turned him into an athlete who was afraid to make mistakes, who walked on eggshells and whose batting average dropped through the floor. An average of .240 is still a pretty decent average in the big leagues, but not nearly what this athlete was capable of.

We worked to help him reconnect with his authentic personality and with his love and passion for the game. The intense stress and pressure he was facing changed his approach to the game and his hitting suffered because of it. Personality changes with changes in stress and pressure. I helped this athlete calm his intensity level down and bring his dynamic personality back into the game. We created an approach to hitting that worked for him and got him reconnected to his approach to the game that he used when he was new in the league. In the last two months of the season he raised his average from .240 to .281, hit 17 home-runs, and 36 RBIs to end the season.

In the next contract year, he was offered a huge contract. He is now a multiple time all-star player in major league baseball. His talent didn't change. The talent was always there. We plugged his personality back into his talent, and the fireworks went off.

That could happen for any of you reading this book. Think about all the times you've shut down, given in, not had a voice or sold yourself out. All the times you have been afraid of making mistakes, afraid of a coach's wrath and input, or tried too hard to get everything perfect.

I once interviewed a bunch of players for the NBA draft, and one player I talked to played for a college coach who pulled him out of the game any time he made a mistake. This guy was playing in a nationally prominent program, but afraid to make a mistake because the minute he did, he got pulled out of the game.

I'm watching one of this guy's college games, and three minutes into the game he makes a turnover; next stop in play he's out of the game. I thought, "He's right. It happens."

I asked him, "How much of your mental and emotional energy is going into basketball? How much of your mental and emotional energy is going into avoiding making mistakes, fear of the coach's wrath, and getting pulled out of the game?" He thought for a minute and then he said, "That's a really good question. Thirty percent basketball and seventy percent avoiding getting taken out of the game, avoiding making mistakes."

I said, "You're a high NBA prospect. If you could take that seventy percent and plug it back into your game what kind of athlete would we be getting?" He said, "The sky's the limit."

Another example, I was talking to a college softball player recently. She told me about all the mind games her coach played on them. She felt lost and confused playing a game she used to love. I asked her, "How much of your energy is going into softball, managing things, trying to figure out what's going to happen next with this coach and avoiding his wrath?"

She said, "Fifteen percent softball and eighty-five percent avoiding his wrath." Under that much stress, under that much pressure, with that much energy being diverted away from the game, there is no way this athlete will ever reach her full potential. That athlete cannot be herself because her brain is stressed, and she is wasting so much energy focusing on the wrong things. She starts the game with what I call a pain-avoiding approach. Instead of playing with love and passion, connection, and loving being out there; she is spending too much energy avoiding mistakes, trying to avoid getting pulled out of the game, and trying to figure out what's going to happen next.

And that doesn't mean it takes a bad coach to make that happen. Many athletes do that to themselves. They make a mistake and then start doing what I call "sliding downhill."

Here's the kicker, I'm going to show you a graph that shows what happens to your energy efficiency when you're performing authentically. Meaning, you're being yourself, you're being congruent, you're being true to who you are and you are pairing your authentic self with your natural talent. The amount of energy you have for performance is remarkable. The amount of effort it takes to be authentic is minimal when we compare it to the amount of energy it takes to be who everyone else wants you to be. The graph also shows you the effect of living in reaction to conditioning, like parents' influence, coaches' influence, or a general manager's influence. The conditioning you put upon yourself with negative thinking and limiting behaviors is called conditioned behavior.

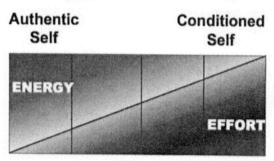

When you're operating from conditioned behavior, you have very low energy, very high effort. So, what we're working on is getting you to be authentic, to be real, to show up empowered, to show up congruent. Take responsibility for your life and your actions and plug that into your talent, and you'll be one of those stories that I talk about all the time.

We just finished a very powerful topic about the importance of personality in performance. Now, I'm going to share with you what I consider to be the three cornerstones that I teach athletes. They will help refine talent and develop skills in sports and in life.

3 PILLARS TO PEAK PERFORMANCE

What I'm going to talk about next is related to sports, and it also relates to life and developing life skills. This segment is called the *"3 Pillars of Peak Performance."* It will help you develop an approach to life that will get you out of being the victim and feeling powerless. It will help you learn how to take responsibility for your life, and take charge of your life and learn how to feel empowered. It will help you free up energy and resources, and help you accomplish so much more on the field, in the pool, in the classroom or any other area of your life.

I learned each of these three pillars at different phases of my life. When I learned them, something in my brain, in my body, and my spirit clicked. Each of these pillars offer an amazing way to approach conflict, struggle, suffering, strife, injury or whatever it might be for you. Let's work our way through these three pillars. I believe you will find them to be life changing.

Again, these are the cornerstones of my practice. I teach these to every athlete that works with me. They might be struggling with different aspects of training performance or being part of a team. They may struggle with parents, coaches or returning from an injury.

If you will start integrating these pillars into your life, they will help you, not just in sports, but also in every part of your life!

Pillar 1 Comfort Zones

"Life begins at the end of the Comfort Zone"
Neil Donald Walsch

The first pillar is recognizing that we all live in comfort zones. A comfort zone is a place that is safe. It's predictable. It's familiar. Our ego likes us there. The part of our brain that wants to keep us safe and familiar and in a routine, likes us there. Athletes, coaches, and parents sometimes tend to settle into comfort zones.

You know you're in a comfort zone when you wake up and do the same thing every day. It's predictable. It's methodical. It's routine. You know you've been in a comfort zone too long when you start feeling bored, melancholy, and your energy is a little bit low.

Breaking out of your comfort zone is the first pillar. What you have to do first is recognize your comfort zone. This is the first step. Mediocrity may be your comfort zone. Financial struggle may be your comfort zone. You can even live in, what I call, an uncomfortable comfort zone.

You could be miserable and suffering. You could be sitting on the bench. You could be competing with not nearly the talent or potential that you're capable of, and yet for some reason you've settled into that comfort zone--that place of familiarity, acceptance, thinking that's just how it's going to be.

One of the things that keep us from moving out of our comfort zone is the fear of failure. If a golfer is having a great round, but he just can't putt that day. What does he do? Does he fold it up and go straight into the 19th hole and have a beer and eat dinner? No, he doesn't. He goes to the practice green and works on his putting because he wants to strengthen the part of his game where he struggled.

If a volleyball player isn't serving well, they might stay after practice and work on their serve. They work on their jump serve, or topspin serve, or float serve, whatever that might be. It takes a mindful athlete to recognize when they are in a comfort zone and begin to work their way back up again.

Athletes experience a lot of success and some horrific failures, then more success and more failure, but eventually they're going to settle into a place that's safe, predictable and familiar. They settle into their comfort zone. Learn how to recognize your comfort zone and ask yourself, "Is this all I've got? Is this the best I can do? Do I want to spend the rest of my life or my career here--wherever here might be, a high school, college, or a professional or elite athlete? Do I want to spend the rest of my time doing this, or do I want to get uncomfortable and step into my greatness?

The way to get out of a comfort zone is to create challenges in your life. For example, if you say, I've been competing at this level for the last two years, and I've decided I want to take my game up to another level. I'm going to challenge myself to move from this double A team to a triple A team by next season.

You might say, "I've been on junior varsity my sophomore year and junior year and by God, I'm going to make it to varsity for my senior year and be the best that I can be."

Maybe you got held back as a level eight gymnast and you want to get out of the comfort zone of being a level eight gymnast. You are going to do whatever it takes to move beyond that comfort zone and get to level nine or ten, if that's where you want to go with it.

Some of what we're talking about sounds like goal setting a little bit and that's part of it, but I'm talking about more than setting goals. I'm specifically talking about the exhibiting behaviors that keep you in a comfort zone or move you out of a comfort zone.

For example, when I was in high school I was a three-sport athlete. I played football, basketball and ran track. I ran hurdles and high jumped with a goal to jump 6'6", run low 14s in the hurdles and mid 38s in the intermediate hurdles.

In the first meet of the season, I jumped 6'6". In the second meet I ran 14.3 in the hurdles, and in the third meet I ran a 38.5 in intermediate hurdles. My times did not improve the rest of the season because the behaviors that I exhibited to jump 6'6", to run a 14.3 and to run a 38.5 stopped.

Once I accomplished those goals, my peak performance behaviors fell off. I didn't reevaluate myself. I didn't do things to continue to set my goals higher and higher, or my behavioral standards higher.

I could have run faster. I could have jumped higher. There are a lot of things that I could have done a lot better.

Sometimes when we set a goal and we rely on that goal, our only focus is that goal or the number of reps or whatever else the goal might be.

We lose our capacity to move far beyond what we're truly capable of performing. To get out of our comfort zone we must ask ourselves, "What part of my personality or what behavior traits do I need to exhibit so that I can move out of my comfort zone and accomplish greatness?" To help you integrate these concepts, start noticing your training regimen, your pre-workout warm-up, your level of competitive intensity, level of focus and level of drive and commitment. You're going to get back what you put into that workout. If you're putting in a high level of energy and focus, you are going to get back a high level of progress and refinement in your performance. Maybe you've settled for being comfortable, but you've got to start challenging yourself to get out of that comfort zone and then you can accomplish more than you thought possible.

I've had athletes that say, "Man, I want to make a national team. Before you know it, they're on the WORLD team. And they're like, "Wow man, I never thought I would make it to the world team." Their character is different. Their personality is different. Their behaviors are different. And the next thing you know they're at Olympic trials.

Some become Olympic athletes and some don't. My point

is, they move way beyond being a national team member. Way beyond where they ever dreamed they could possibly go. So, **Pillar #1** is getting out of your comfort zone.

Pillar #2 Stop taking things personally.

Take everything that you face as a challenge. This approach gets you out of the trap of being a victim whenever things get tough. It improves your ability to rise to challenges. I've worked with athletes who came to see me because they have a teammate that's bullying them or causing problems. Maybe another athlete is getting a little bit more playing time or a little more attention from the coach.

"The time when there is no one there to feel sorry for you or to cheer for you is when the player is made."

Tim Duncan.

You can suffer with that. You can struggle with that. You can be the victim, or you can face the challenge head on and in the process, develop parts of your personality you might never have been able to access without the challenge.

I worked with two NFL players who were very talented, but in the NFL draft, management brought high drafted players to take their positions.

We talked at length about their choices in how they

handled this. They could handle it like a victim and think, "They don't care about me. Poor me. What am I going to do? What if I get cut?" Or, they can handle it as an important challenge in their careers. Their thinking might be "It's on! I'm going to show my team that I'm the guy. I'm the right person. I'm the right one to lead this team or play this position."

One of these players signed with a new team and became one of the best at his position in the league. He led his team to one of their best seasons in years. The other player also found a new team, signed a nice contract and became one of the best at his position.

This approach gets you out of being a victim. It empowers you. Athletes that are not empowered and feel like victims do not perform very well. They never meet their full potential.

Empowered athletes are athletes who take responsibility, maximize talent, maximize potential, who consistently compete at very, very high levels. Stop taking things personally. Take everything as a challenge. It doesn't matter if it's an interaction with the coach, an interaction with the media, a teammate or an injury that you sustained. You wouldn't believe how many athletes have actually told me, "I never thought I'd say this, but I'm glad the injury happened. I took it on as a challenge, and it changed my life. I'm not the same person since the injury that I was before. I'm fierce, I'm more determined, I have more faith."

They took the injury as a challenge. They rose to the challenge and responded magnificently. **Pillar #2** stop taking things personally. Take everything as a challenge and rise to that challenge.

Pillar #3 On some level I brought this to me How can I grow from this experience?"

"Persistence can change failure into extraordinary achievement."
Matt Biondi

Again, this keeps us from being a victim. I've had some very frustrating and upsetting things happen in my work with teams and organizations. I have worked my tail off on teams that I thought would make remarkable things happen, and things just didn't go as planned. There was sabotage, or ego, or injuries, and other things that happened that derailed that team's potential. These distractors got in the way of something I had poured my heart and soul into. When that happened, I thought, "I can be a victim to this" or I can think, "Alright, it's happening now. I've brought this to me so on some level. I'm ready for this. How can I grow from this experience? What could I have done differently that might have stopped this from happening, or what can I do in the future that will prevent this from happening again."

I was in one organization where we had a lot of success, but after my relationship with that organization ended, I happened to find some research that said you must have ten factors in place to be successful in an organization. These factors included the freedom to implement your product, backing of leadership, belief by the key players and on and on and on. I realized that I only had three of the ten. Even though I had only three of the ten in place, I still accomplished some remarkable things doing my job with this organization. Did it end? Yes. Was I upset when it ended? Yes, but all things end. They say every athlete retires someday or every relationship ends or changes at some point. I learned that when I agree to work with an organization, I want to have nine or ten of those factors in place, and some of them are critical. So, it happened, I brought it to me. I learned. I've grown from the experience. It was remarkable. The whole ride was remarkable and I'm better for it. The experience helped me build character, credibility and faith in my services.

To recap, get out of your comfort zone, stop taking things personally. Take everything as a challenge, and if it's happening now, I'm ready for it. How can I grow from these experiences?

If you implement these 3 pillars into your life as an athlete, as a young man or woman, a parent, a coach, or whatever part of our culture you're in, I'm telling you that life is going to get easier. It's going to help make all the other concepts about peak performance zones, and managing energy and resources become second nature. You'll become so much more efficient in the way you approach life, and most importantly, you'll keep fanning the flames of passion that are so vital to performance.

We're going to move into another topic that I have a lot of passion about. Understanding the mental and emotional impact of serious sports related injuries.

THE MENTAL AND EMOTIONAL IMPACT OF SPORTS INJURIES

In this chapter, we're talking about the mental and emotional impact of sports related injuries. This isn't something that I read in a book or just happened upon. My passion for this topic comes from a lifetime of learning about injuries; experiencing sports injuries and helping athletes overcome the mental and emotional impact of injuries.

It all started for me back when I was in the 7th grade. I had a remarkable growth spurt where I grew eight or nine inches in a year, and I grew so fast that I was in danger of tearing the patellar tendon away from my tibia/fibula. It's called Osgood-Schlatter's disease. I missed all sports that year-- football, basketball, and track. My parents were going through a horrendous divorce, and I didn't have sports to lean on. I wasn't part of a team. I didn't have that outlet which was a part of my identity, and all that began knocking me off course somewhat. In the 9th grade, I separated my left shoulder, broke my right arm and had a concussion.

The big one for me came when I was a sophomore in high school. I was covering a kickoff at the end of the regular season. We were a state-ranked football team, and I had just moved from defensive back to defensive end, and I was playing the best football of my life. A guy hit me on opening kickoff. I tore three ligaments, the medial meniscus, strained the patellar tendon, and ruptured the fluid capsule in my knee. Back then, it was a really bad injury, but nobody bothered to tell me that. So, I had surgery, which resulted in my leg in a cast for six weeks.

Back then rehab was -- two saw horses, a piece of plywood, some plumber's pipe and a belt, and all I did was leg extensions for months and month and months. There wasn't anything about range of motion or strengthening abductors and adductors or any of that stuff. I got my quad strong and remarkably I was back nine months later which, for that kind of an injury back in the dark ages of surgery in the 70's, I think it's pretty miraculous.

I wasn't the same athlete, though. I was terrified of hurting that knee again, so as a result I suffered other injuries. I separated my right shoulder. I had another concussion. I was hesitant--very, very passive.

I went to college and tried to play sports, but in the spring, the athletic trainer came up to me and said, "You need to stop worrying about hurting your knee again." I kind of bowed up and said, "I'm fine." But I knew he got me. I just didn't realize it was that obvious.

In the spring game I separated my left shoulder *again* and that's when I decided to hang it up. I'd had enough of injuries. I ended up working in oil and gas, then investment banking before I got a calling to go back to graduate school and get a Master's degree in Psychology. In graduate school, my area of focus was post-traumatic stress disorder, researching trauma.

My master's thesis was on trauma, research was on trauma, as well as presentations and papers. After graduate school, I did a lot of extensive training with Eye Movement Desensitization and Reprocessing (EMDR), eidetic imagery, re-scripting, and trauma resolution.

Many years ago, it kind of hit me that the same work I was doing with people involved in fatal and near fatal automobile accidents, bank robberies and mountain climbing accidents, would help injured athletes overcome the psychological, mental and emotional impact of their sports related injuries.

So, I called a buddy of mine, Steve VanMeter, who is a high school athletic director and head football coach, and I took him out for lunch. I worked my way through the timeline of an injury from the onset of an injury, to the examination, all the way through surgery and coming back to play again.

Then I asked him, "During that process, does an athlete go through any stress, sadness, grief, anger, resentment, bitterness, whatever that might be?"

And he said, "Yeah, the whole gamut. All my injured athletes experience those feelings."

I asked, "Who's helping them?"

He replied, "Nobody's doing that. What are *you* talking about?"

"That's what I want to do. That's my next mission. That's the vision that I have for me in my life."

He sent me my first athlete, a kid who had torn his ACL in a scrimmage the year before. His team was about to scrimmage the same team again, and this kid was terrified of getting hurt. I'm sure many of you can identify with that. You are coming back from an ACL injury, a Tommy John, a broken ankle, or something like that, and there's this part of your brain that's focused on, maybe even been obsessing,

"Am I going to get hurt again?" You even might see images in your mind of your knee buckling again or throwing a curve ball and your elbow popping again.

I went to work with this kid and four or five sessions later, he was a different player. I went back to watch him play at that scrimmage because he was playing at my old high school in Friendswood, Texas, and this kid was a beast. He was just dominant. His offensive line play was awesome, and after the scrimmage was over his mother came up to me and said, "I don't know what you did with my son, but there was no fear. It was a God-thing." And I believe that.

I think what we did was a very, very powerful thing for this young man. It was not just his athletic career; it was his life. That set me off on this journey with a mission of helping as many injured athletes as I can to come back from the psychological, mental and emotional impact of sports related injuries.

Now, let's look at what happens in an injury. Let's say, for example, an athlete is running down the field and makes a cut, a soccer player makes a cut, and they tear their ACL. Athletes that I work with have some image in their mind of that moment in time.

They remember, "I'm lying on the field. I hear the pop. I feel the pop. I'm holding my knee."

Another image might be, "I'm sitting on the sidelines with

my trainer. They have ice on my knee. I can see the team doctor looking at my trainer and saying the words ACL." These are all very, very vivid images and memories that I hear from athletes over and over repeatedly.

Another example is the soccer player who goes into a 50/50 ball and somebody slides in and breaks their ankle. They can remember looking down and seeing their ankle hanging in a strange angle, or maybe they remember the next morning when their ankle is five times its regular size and it's purple, yellow and black.

These are called holographic imprints or holographic images. When an injury happens, the brain starts firing, taking these pictures and loading the images with emotion, pain, sound, smell, perception and more. Meanwhile, the athlete is injured and they go through the examination process by the team athletic trainer or the team doctor.

If it's a bad injury, there's a follow-up visit to an orthopedic surgeon or someone who specializes in shoulder injuries, arm injuries or knee injuries. If it's an ACL injury it might take a couple of weeks to let the swelling go down and then they go into surgery. They have the surgery; they come out of surgery and start the rehab process. They do the rehab work and the athlete comes back to play sports once they're cleared by their physician and they live happily ever after. Right?

No! That's not how it always works. Through that whole process, the part of the brain that is designed to keep us safe and keep us alive is engaged. It's called the limbic system. The limbic system regulates emotion.

There's a part of the brain called the amygdala. When the amygdala starts firing, it freaks out, especially with an injury. The part of the brain that regulates the concepts of time and memory is also a part of the limbic system. When you get those three parts of the brain engaged, it lights up. The limbic system begins to draw energy from the parts of the brain that have to do with passion and focus and connection to your sport.

So, these athletes go through the current treatment model, which focuses on the surgery, getting them to rehab and then returning them to play.

There's not a lot of consideration put into what happens with an athlete in the moment of injury. What happens when they're lying in bed at home for three days and they can't move and they start having questions about their future?

"Will I ever be the same? Will my knee be the same? What if someone takes my position? What if they take away my college scholarship?"

I worked with a guy a few years ago who had 26 Division-One college scholarship offers. In a 7-on-7 football tournament, he tore his knee up bad. Twenty-six college scholarships went away! The kid was devastated when he found his way to me. I helped him with his comeback. He ended up having to give up the sport because it was a very bad injury. When we began our work together he was depressed, lonely, disconnected, not involved in school. We addressed his injury, his loss of scholarships, the loss of his identity, his loss of the love and connection to teammates and the sport he loved. After our work together he enrolled in college, his depression lifted, he found another sport he could channel his passion into. He was happy again. His old personality came back.

Many people, including doctors, coaches, athletic trainers and parents don't fully understand this paradigm. The good news is that the paradigm is changing. More and more providers, coaches, athletes and parents see the importance and the power of working through the mental and emotional impact of serious sports related injuries. There's a lot going on with these injuries. You have to look at the fears of going into surgery. Rational fears versus irrational fears. I will explain the difference. Then there's the pain because of the surgery that creates an imprint in the brain. They remember it as a huge mental and emotional incident in their lives.

After surgery and going through the pain, they start the rehab process. There's uncertainty there too, because they might only be able to fire their quad for five seconds at a time and that's their workout for the day. Some athletes must learn to walk again or learn how to throw again. They start throwing from 20 feet, and they get back on the mound in six, eight or nine months. It's a very, very slow process. It is very taxing mentally and emotionally. It challenges them. Then they come back to play and often there's this impactful fear of re-injury that comes up.

Many athletes, their head coaches and their parents might say, "Well, they're a head case. They're just not the same athlete." Injuries do that to athletes. They change their personality and the way an athlete approaches sports. My passion is helping athletes validate what they've been through; helping them put a language to that because a lot of athletes get quiet. They don't know how to put words to what they have been through. An injured athlete might become very quiet and withdrawn.

I worked with a girl years ago that had torn her ACL. Before her injury, she always walked around the house singing. Her parents brought her to me a year after she had surgery and one of the things they told me was, "She's not herself."

I asked them, "What's different?"

They replied, "She's not as happy. She doesn't seem to be as spontaneous as she used to be. She doesn't sing anymore. We always loved hearing her singing around the house, and she doesn't do that anymore."

And so, they brought her in and we went to work to find out what her triggers were. What upsetting memories and images did we need to work on? In a few short sessions, this girl was back to her old self. The most satisfying thing for me was when her mother called me and said, "You're not going to believe what happened today."

I said, "What's that?"

She replied, "My daughter came down stairs today, and she was singing again. We haven't heard her sing in a year." It was a pretty emotional moment for both of us.

I believe we are helping injured athletes reclaim that dynamic, vital personality that's so important to performance. The way we help is to first identify the triggers that their brain has locked on to that are connected to the injury. The holographic images in the brain are when the brain takes snapshots of the worst part of the injury experience. It may be an image of you standing on the sidelines watching someone else do your job, or it may be an image of you watching your team make a long run in the playoffs while you sit on the sidelines.

Or, it could be an image of you watching somebody else get that contract you thought was yours. Another image might be of you having a conversation with the general manager that they are letting you go. "It's a tough business, and we're letting you go because you are not the same player you were before you got injured." I'm sure some of you can relate to these stories.

With the athletes I coach, I find out what the brain is struggling to process. What are the critical moments? What are the formative moments? Your brain takes these images and files away the emotions. It files away physical sensations in the body. It files away pain.

I worked with a guy that played football for the University of Michigan and hurt his knee. When he was being carried off the field, he could smell brats cooking in the concession stands. That was a very vivid part of his holographic imprint.

I had a gymnast that I worked with who got disoriented on a high bar release skill. He remembers the lights in the arena and the name of the company that made the mats coming up at his face very, very quickly as he was heading down towards the bar. He ended up with a pretty serious head injury. This stored information in the limbic system just sits there. It's like a storm or a hurricane.

The image sits there swirling and turning, and when the athlete goes back out to throw another off-speed pitch after they have torn their Tommy John, or they go to make a cut, or they go after that 50-50 ball as a soccer player, or in the case of the gymnast, tries that same release skill on high bar; all of the stored information is activated on a pretty intense level. The part of the brain that holds this memory and is trying to keep the athlete from being injured again kicks in and says, "I'm going to do my job here and I'm not going to let you get hurt again."

At that, the athlete tries but just can't perform the skills at the level they were before the event. That doesn't mean that every athlete needs the kind of treatment I provide, but I am convinced that a high percentage of them do. I am certain that every injured athlete could benefit on some level from going through this injury protocol.

With changes in modern medicine, rehab and physical therapy, athletes make remarkable recoveries and return to play sooner. They might be stronger physically, but with the rehab process taking less time, there's less time for the brain to process the mental and emotional issues or the impact of the injury.

ACL injuries used to require a year to a year and a half for full recovery and return to play. I'm talking to athletes now who are coming back in seven or eight months. So that's five, six even seven months of time that the brain doesn't have to process, integrate and file away traumatic images, memories, emotions and other stressful information associated with the injury.

Treating the rational and irrational fears that injured athletes have prior to surgery is another critical component to complete recovery from sports injuries. For example, I asked one athlete, prior to surgery, "When you think about surgery, what do you think about?"

He replied, "I just see my leg sliced open and the doctor cutting my knee up."

"I have a fear that they are not giving me enough anesthesia. I'm out, but I'm not all the way out. I can feel everything they're doing, and nobody knows I can feel it."

Or, "I have this irrational fear that they are going to operate on the wrong leg," or "What if they cut the wrong ligament and I can't play sports anymore."

These are all actual stories I hear repeatedly. Seeing an athlete prior to surgery is a game changer. Once we mentally and emotionally prepare them for surgery, the limbic system is not engaged going into surgery, so the brain is not producing stress related hormones. The athlete goes into surgery calmer.

I've had athletes come back and say, "The nurse asked me if I had surgery before because I seemed so calm." They approach surgery with more confidence, less anxiety and much less fear. They tend to experience less pain after the surgical procedure. When we meet again a few weeks after surgery, we start working on what happened with the play when they got hurt. We work on the injury itself and all the events surrounding it, including being taken to the emergency room, carted off the field, or whatever that might be. We especially work on the actual play where they were injured.

They return to play with a new vision and experience of what 100 percent ready to return truly is. It's a new definition of 100 percent. The physical, mental and emotional components of the injury have been addressed and they're ready to go.

Then we do what I call cleanup work. We work through any residual issues that need to be addressed to help them feel totally confident. I saw a female soccer player who had been cleared to return to play. She came to see me because she found out her first game back was going to be at the same field where she suffered her knee injury. She said she was feeling anxious and had a bad image in her mind of the part of the field where she was hurt. We processed that negative information, and she went out and played a great match with no issues whatsoever. I usually hear, "I don't even think about my knee anymore. It's not even a concern, and I don't see those images in my head anymore. I'm ready to go."

Injured athletes can learn so much about themselves in the process of overcoming an injury. Injuries can be life changing in a negative way, but if you're willing to do what I call "mine the gold" from these experiences and learn about yourself, injuries can allow you to find a part of your personality that you might never have accessed. That part of you that is more courageous, fiercer, more determined and more focused. One specific attribute I observe with injured athletes I work with is the ability to be patient during the return to play process. They must remember that every day is a day that you are getting better, and they have to learn how to think long term. I hope it's obvious that I have a lot of passion about sports-related injuries.

This injury work is phenomenal. If the things I say hit home with you, or if you know of someone who can benefit from this approach to sports injury recovery, please contact me. We can get you back in the game again with passion, with confidence and a true connection to the sport you love.

In the next chapter, we're going to talk about parenting athletes.

This is great information. Parents, I know it will help you do a better job of empowering your athletes.

PARENTING ATHLETES AND ENJOYING THE JOURNEY

"Your child's success or lack of success in sports does not indicate what kind of parent you are. But, having an athlete that is coachable, respectful, a great teammate, mentally tough, resilient, and tries their best is a direct reflection of your parenting"
Unknown

This segment is for parents—parents of athletes. It is also for the athletes. Get ready to learn a lot about the importance and power of parenting an athlete. I have two kids who are athletes. My daughter is a volleyball player, and my son is a baseball player. I have been watching them, coaching them, sitting in the stands since they were four years old, and they are a lot older than that now. So I've had my successes, and I've had my struggles as a parent. I can laugh at myself about some of it and some of it is like "I did what?"

We've all done that. We've all been there. I'm going to teach you some things that I've learned through my own experiences of parenting athletes and from the many parents who come up and approach me in the stands. They ask questions like, "Can you sit down and tell me what I can do to help with this situation?"

"My son or my daughter or my athlete is doing this and I'm reacting. What could help me?"

I felt like it was important to capture this information and talk about it, so that you can learn some really powerful lessons. Learn what you can do to, not only help your athlete be better, but help you enjoy this process and this journey. Many times we get focused on the outcome or the goal. But, if you're not enjoying the process and the journey, you're missing out on so much. Even the struggles can turn into teachable moments and victories for the entire family.

My kids have been through ups and downs. They have struggled at times. I always tell them and other athletes I work with that the right way to approach the struggle is to go through it, not around it. The gift for me, as a parent, is not so much how they play the game, but who they are and who they become in this process of being an athlete. Thank God I've learned from my experiences. I've learned from my struggles, and I want to share what I have learned with you. I'm not perfect as a parent, but I have learned a lot in 20 plus years of parenting athletes.

The first concept for me, in the athlete's system, is what I call the "3-legged stool." In junior high, high school, college, it's the athlete, the coach (or the coach's system), and the parents. As you move further along in sports, there's more to it. There is a general manager or there might be an agent. There are various other players, so the legs get more complicated. There are more legs involved in the process.

For simplicity's sake, we're going to talk about the 3-legged stool today, because I'm not talking about general managers in this process. I'm talking to you as parents, so let's go with the 3-legged stool--the athlete, the coach or the coaches, and parents.

If you sit down on a 3-legged stool and all 3 legs are strong and intact, you feel comfortable sitting on that stool, right? It feels sturdy. If there's weakness in anyone of those legs it makes the whole system, the whole support structure, shaky and vulnerable.

I'm talking about what we can do to make you a better parent, make you more empathetic and help you understand what your athlete goes through during training and competition. You're strengthening your leg on the 3-legged stool, and you're going to help strengthen your athlete's leg. That's huge just in itself.

In the Athlete's Assessment, one of the first segments in this book, I asked your athlete to talk about, write down and journal about themselves when they're at their absolute best. They talked about being passionate, plugged in, inspired, unstoppable, having fun and locked in.

Then I have them take a deep breath and write down what it's like when they're struggling as an athlete. Now they talk about suffering, being angry, shutting down, having low confidence and not having fun. These are two athletes--right? Well guess what, there are a couple of different parents sitting in the stands when it comes to sports performance.

If you want to get a piece of paper and a pen, let's do the same exercise with you, the parent. What are you like at your best as a parent? You're sitting in the stands watching your son or daughter swim, or you're at the baseball or softball field, or you're at a track meet. You are sitting in the stands during a volleyball, football, soccer, golf or fencing. You are at your best as a parent! You encourage, motivate and inspire. You are proud, plugged in, supportive and passionate. We could go on and on. That's usually what I hear from parents at their best, right? Take a few minutes and write that down.

Capture that information because that is the person we want sitting in the stands consistently.

Now, switch places in your mind. Write down, "me at my worst as a parent." This might be tough. This is where you must be honest with yourself. If you want to get better you must be real. "I'm belligerent. I'm controlling. It's all about me. I'm angry. I'm blaming. I'm reactive. I don't know how to control my emotions. I get up and walk away when they compete poorly. I abandon them." Sadly, I hear that too often.

The truth is, both parents exist in each of us. Just like there's a best athlete and a struggling athlete, there's you at your best and you when you're struggling. It happens to all of us.

I have done parent workshops where I've had one parent stand up and say remarkably vulnerable things about what they've done with their kids. How they reacted to their kids! How they responded! It changes the whole dynamic in the room because it gives everyone else permission to be real. You just wouldn't believe where we can go with these workshops when parents are being real. It's profound, the vulnerability and openness is something you can feel in the room.

We change paradigms in a high school basketball workshop or a swim club or wherever it is we're showing up.

When parents are vulnerable, they are open. That's what I am asking of you as you do this exercise. Own it! Be vulnerable. Take responsibility.

I am going to give you some tools to help you start this process of change so you can enjoy the game and enjoy watching your athlete even more. An athlete's performance changes based on pressure they feel. It's plain and simple. Performance shifts when changes occur in thinking, perception and attitude. Well guess what, those same things affect you as a parent, too. Pressure pushes in on you and you change the way you parent.

When you come home from work and you've had a really bad day, you might come in and go straight upstairs to hide and watch TV. You might get angry, or you might look at doing something else, like having a few drinks to de-stress. You might become controlling or run around and turn off lights or clean the house. The point is, your personality (and behavior) changes with changes in stress and pressure. Earlier we talked about your athlete learning how to consistently stay in their *peak performance zone*. By this, I mean learning how to stay in a zone that maximizes their talent and potential.

Parents have what I call the *peak enjoyment zone* and that means being in a right place mentally, emotionally, spiritually and physically. They are present to enjoy the ups and downs, the good and bad. When it comes to sports, there is really no failure. It's all learning. If you can't handle your kids struggle and failure, then you are really robbing your kids in the process of learning through sports. Learning is one of the most powerful gifts that sports brings to us and to our kids-- the process of learning how to overcome adversity, struggle and failure, and then growing from these experiences. The more time you spend in your *peak enjoyment zone*, the better the whole environment is going to be and the stronger that 3-legged stool will be.

You play a very important part in this process. Don't underestimate that. Kids are like little lightning rods or tuning forks. They pick up on everything you do. I have athletes tell me they can feel their parents in the stands; they can hear their voices in the stands. They tell me they saw their mom and dad get up and leave "when I struck out" or "when I fell on the ice."

"Out of the corner of my eye I saw them get up and leave." They are in tune with everything that goes on, consciously or unconsciously. The unconscious is 90 percent of our brainpower. Your kids are feeling even more of what you do than they are aware of. Consciously and unconsciously they take in your behaviors, your antics, your emotions, your comments, and they define their personality and self-confidence around you the parent and how you show up in the stands.

I want to talk about what happens in the car ride home or at dinner between games--some do's and don'ts. This *peak enjoyment zone* is critical. With the athletes we talked a lot about mindfulness, as parents it is time for you to also become mindful. Be aware of what you are doing when you are doing it. Notice yourself. "I notice I'm sitting on the edge of my seat. I notice I'm getting agitated. I notice I'm standing up and clapping. I notice I'm getting angry. I notice I'm yelling, "Come on Blue!" "What was that?"

Recognize when you are starting to get out of your *peak enjoyment zone*

I've talked with athletes about developing an internal GPS system that helps them recognize when they are getting off-center. Parents, we do it too. We get off center mentally and emotionally, too. Learn how to recognize when you are getting off course, when you are starting to bring behavior into the environment in a way that is not life giving. These negative behaviors are what I call tank *draining* instead of tank *filling* behaviors.

Be mindful. Learn to be aware. Take ownership of that awareness and take corrective action. I have been at my daughter's volleyball match when things just weren't going well, and I felt those behaviors coming on that I don't like. I have a Fit Bit that I wear all the time. I get up and walk around the arena, and I knock out about 2000 steps. And then I go back and sit down. I feel better. I changed my perspective. Get up and walk! Stand up and breathe! Switch places. Do something different to get you out of that place.

Another thing you can do is what I call "clean house." That means if you see a big competition on the horizon, tie up your loose ends. Get your ducks in a row. Take care of business so you won't go into the critical tryout for volleyball or a golf team too amped up or agitated. Your kid might have Olympic aspirations. You could go to Olympic trials, and you're frazzled because you have this project coming down the pipe that you haven't started because you have been so focused on your son or daughter's progress to national, world and Olympic team trials. I've been there with a number of parents who had to take care of their business, clean house and tie up loose ends. Solve problems before they ever become problems. If you can't solve the problem or clean the house, leave it at home. Make it a ritual to mentally and emotionally leave the stress behind you so you can be totally present and in the moment.

I worked with a college football player who was a punter. His parents would tell him about a lot of their problems and other stressful things going on. This athlete got really, really stressed out about things going on at home and couldn't separate home from performance. He was thinking, "What if I don't perform well?" "What if I lose my scholarship?"

There was a ton of negativity swirling around him.

First, I taught him how to talk to his parents so they didn't get inside that bubble of his, that sacred space for competing and training. That space needs to be an oxygen-rich environment, a life-giving environment. He taught them, "I don't want to hear about financial problems. I don't want to hear about other problems of yours. I'm here to do a job. I'm here to get an education." They honored that. They listened.

I taught him this ritual. When he got off the team bus and began walking to the stadium, I asked him to pick up a rock. As he walked through the stadium into the locker room, he squeezed all the stress, anxiety and worry into that rock. Then he put the rock on top of his locker with his shoes. Mentally he left everything in the locker room. And then he went out and played the game--absent of all that stress and absent of his parent's negativity. This kid became a national leader in punting. He was able to get rid of his distractions by teaching his parents how he wanted to be treated as their son and as an athlete. When the game was over, he went into the locker room, took a shower and got dressed. He took that rock and on the way to the team bus, dropped it back into the place where he found it. It was a ritual that we created to help him let go of stress, and it worked for him. I've taught that to many athletes.

In my family we have, what I call, the two-hour rule. What

that means is, you can't talk about anything negative for at least two hours after the event, the performance or the game.

During those two hours, everything is always positive. Why? First, it gives you, the parent, time to decompress, so you don't blast them like a flamethrower with your negativity. Second, it gives your athlete time to process. They need time to think about it, integrate it and work their way through it. Third, athletes are usually harder on themselves than you'll ever be and they don't need anything extra piling up on them.

After that two hours, you get to decide if you want to talk to them about their performance, or not. We used to have a two-hour rule in my family, now we have a 24-hour rule. Most of the time we don't even talk about it. Our kids know what they need to do. They know what adjustments to make and most of the time are able to make those changes themselves. Sometimes they will ask me, "Hey, can I talk to you about such and such?" or I'll sit down and say, "How do you feel about the way you played?" I never say, "Why did you do this?" It's always, "How do you feel about that game?"

"Well, my serving was great. My fastball was on. I couldn't get my curveball working". We talk. We process it. It is never pile drive them into the ground. I've heard horror stories of tennis players getting into their cars with their parents after a match and people walking by could hear the yelling and the shouting going on inside the car. The sad thing is that these parents think that screaming and yelling really help to make their kid a better athlete. Honest to God, that's a true story. Or, parents making kids walk home because they perform so poorly. Really!!!

That wouldn't work for me. It wouldn't work in my family, and I don't think it's going to work for you in your family either. In addition to this two-hour rule, don't talk about the coach in front of your kids. Minimize it if you can and don't talk about other players. If you do, make it good and positive. What happens if you start trash talking the coach and, "Why is he doing this? And he doesn't know what he's talking about. He always plays his favorites." Then your child, your athlete, learns to see that coach through your eyes and through your lens of perception. They don't see them through their own heart, mind and eyes anymore. They only see them through your perception. Minimize talking about coaches and other players. It is terribly damaging to your athlete. It creates toxicity and hurts that oxygen rich, life-giving bubble where we want them training and competing.

You also must look at what things set you off. What are your triggers? Athletes have triggers--making a mistake, a bad call, a bad score and things like that. Things will happen during your athlete's competition that will trigger you. They will set you off and bring out that "worst parent." You have to look at the areas that you are vulnerable. What pokes at you and pushes your buttons?

Learn how to breathe. Belly breathing is a very powerful technique for athletes, and it is a very powerful technique for parents. Use diaphragmatic breathing! Make your stomach go out and your diaphragm go down. Your lungs expand and that sends a message to your brain to relax, calm down. Take five or six deep breaths when you feel yourself starting to get frustrated or angry. Breathe. Be mindful. Calm yourself down. I said previously, get up and move. Get up and walk around a little bit. Switch seats or talk to somebody else--whatever works.

Also, reward your child's effort not their results. Results are a part of that destination process. To only reward results undermines all the hard work that your athlete has put into their sport--the sacrifices and the commitments.

I tell my kids "I'm so proud of how hard you worked to get here. I'm so proud of the efforts that you showed this weekend in the tournament. I'm so proud of you." Whether they played great or didn't play great. Reward the effort. It fills their tanks.

If your acknowledgement is all based on performance, or results, they start looking to you. They read your energy level, your affirmation or your displeasure. "Did I do good or bad?" If they've given great effort, reward the effort. Praise the effort.

I talked earlier about the GPS system. This GPS system is just like the one you have in your car, or on your phone. You punch in a destination. You want to go from Point A to Point B. Every time you get off the course the GPS *reroutes* you. You can *reroute* yourself with all the things that I've been talking about, but it takes mindfulness. It takes self-awareness. It takes learning how to breathe the right way. Resolve your loose ends, solve your problems, be aware and get into your *peak enjoyment zone.*

Bring yourself back into balance again.

I hope these suggestions help you become a better parent for your athlete. Most importantly, I hope they help you enjoy the game more.

Speaking of parents, I get many calls from parents and their athletes concerned about mental blocks in sports. We are going to cover that in depth in the next segment.

OVERCOMING MENTAL BLOCKS IN SPORTS

I think this subject is a fascinating and remarkable topic in the world of sports. I am talking about what we call *mental blocks*. It doesn't really matter whether you're a gymnast, cheerleader, pole-vaulter, golfer, or any other athlete. It maybe you are a baseball player, or the catcher that can't throw the ball back to the pitcher.

I see it all the time. I get calls from parents and athletes alike. It's almost beyond belief. I wrote an article years ago about *mental blocks* and with the power of the Internet, the article went out all over the place. I received calls from New York to California and Florida, all the way to Alaska and all points in between, "My son, my daughter, they're struggling with this mental block. What can we do? What can we do?

I want to get this information out so you can have a better understanding of what's going on. Many athletes who are struggling with mental blocks have parents, coaches or teammates that say, "Just throw the ball! Just jump! Just go up on the pole vault! Just hit the golf ball, or throw the baseball or softball back to the pitcher."

They don't understand that there's a part of the brain that just won't let that happen. The brain won't let that happen because of stress or traumatic experiences or both. A part of the brain gets engaged and says, "No, it ain't going to happen."

The reason this *mental block* happens is, first, the brain has a job to do. One part of the brain has a job to do called "keep you safe." The second reason for the *mental block* is the brain saying, "You've got too much going on. If you don't take care of this or until you take care of it, I'm not going to let you perform this specific skill or activity."

I'm going to expand on this because this is the same kind of introductory concepts where you start thinking about "causes." When an athlete comes to me for help, the first place I look is, "Has there been any serious injuries or falls with this athlete?" It could be a pole-vaulter who goes up and comes down and breaks his ankle, or tears his ACL, or hits his head on the box. It could be the gymnast who goes up to work on a series of backward skills on the floor, gets disoriented, comes down, lands on his or her head or neck, and it scares the bejeebers out of them.

It could be a cheerleader. It's the same thing. They're the flyer, or they do certain tumbling skills, and they get dropped or they fall or get disoriented.

It could be a baseball catcher. One spring season I worked with 13 baseball and softball catchers from high school, college and professional leagues that were all having a hard time throwing the ball back to the pitcher. They had to walk the ball out or lob the ball back, and it was embarrassing and tough on them. They wanted to throw the ball but couldn't, no matter how hard they tried there was still that hesitation, that funny hitch in their motion, or they flat out couldn't throw.

It could be the golfer who stands over the ball, waggling and waggling. It shows up all over the place--tumblers, ice skaters that twist uncontrollably or can't twist at all.

As you can see, I have seen this in all different sports. I take a careful look at their injury history because serious falls and injuries tend to activate the limbic system easily. In most cases of mental blocks, there is some type of serious incident--injuries, bad falls, accidents, car wrecks, family deaths, abusive coaches or parents, bullying or a serious illness that has activated the part of the brain that causes the block.

The second place I look is stressors. What's going on in their life right now that's overloading their brain? I had a call from someone out of state about their daughter, and they were willing to bring their daughter to Houston to see me. I sent them the stress worksheet--same one that we did on managing stress and energy in a previous chapter.

This athlete had things on the worksheet that had to do with graduating from senior high school, completing college applications, prom, finishing up school work, wanting to make the State meet her last year of gymnastics, and a teammate who was always hiding her grips and getting her in trouble. All these stressors added up and when they totaled their stress score it was extremely high.

When they came in the office and I asked, "How was your stress worksheet?" Her first comment was, "I had no idea I was so stressed out." So what that means is, unconsciously they're just plowing through with these stressors, trying to cope with them. They are utilizing too many of the brain's resources in this process, and their brain finally says, "Enough." Many times, when athletes check things off the stress list and take care of business, they get rid of their stressors, their stress score drops, their brain focuses on the skill they want to execute and the brain says, "Thank you very much! I'll let you tumble now. I'll let you throw a baseball. I'll let you throw a softball. I'll let you spin or flip or twirl, or pole vault or whatever it is that you have been struggling with."

It's called the Diathesis-Stress Model. For whatever reason there's a predisposition for this *block*. It could be genetics. They could come from a family with a long line of anxiety. There could be a lot of intensity or fear in your family, or with your team, or school, or whatever that might be.

The predisposition lies dormant, it takes a certain level of stress, fear, anxiety or pressure for the predisposition to kick in. If it's a very high predisposition or tendency, it doesn't take very much stress at all. If it is a very low predisposition, it takes a whole lot of stress. This is why it is so important for athletes to manage stress, get adequate sleep, eat well, stay hydrated and keep their stress scores low.

I had a call this week from the mother of a girl that I work with. Her mother said, "She's been doing great, but she's starting to struggle again. She's starting to have these mental blocks show up again." I sent them the stress worksheet. I said, "Something happened to cause the stress levels to get intense, and intense enough for the predisposition to kick back in again. Sure enough, she emailed me and said, "It's the end of school, finals, getting ready to move up a grade, trying out for a higher-level team, so those stressors kicked in. The symptom, the mental block, showed up again.

The 3rd thing I look for is past high-stress events. I had a baseball catcher that I worked with who was a D1 recruit, very talented kid, and "all of a sudden" he couldn't throw a baseball back to the pitcher. We looked at past injuries, falls and other stressful events. We couldn't find anything that was really pushing in on this kid and causing problems and kicking in the Diathesis-Stress Model.

In his third session, he goes, "Oh you probably need to know I was in a really bad car wreck a while back. I wonder if that has anything to do with it."

I asked, "When was the car wreck?"

He said, "Last November."

I said, "When did the throwing issue start?"

And he goes, "Wow, right around Thanksgiving. How about that?" We connected the dots, went back and did some work around the car wreck. The kid is throwing the baseball back again with no problems.

I had an athlete that I was working with recently who had *mental blocks* in their sport. We sourced it back to something that happened ten years ago. He made a bad throw during a critical inning of a game. He was raged at by his coach and then his father on the way home. Whenever he was stressed and it was a pressure situation in a game, he tended to make bad throws. His brain had created a neurological imprint around the original incident with his coach and father. When we resolved the original event, he had no more throwing issues.

Sometimes I've had parents or athletes call me and I'll say, "How long has this been going on?" Two years, three years, four years? These can be really tough cases and here's why. The brain files information away by outrageousness, intensity, how much emotion is brought into the experience, pain, consequences, and most importantly repetition. The longer an incident goes on, the more its repeated, the deeper the neurological imprinting and the deeper the pathway in the brain. The greater the likelihood the athlete will experience *mental blocks*. When an athlete is overloaded with stress, injuries, traumatic experiences, or experiences that overload their brain, the neurological pathway in the brain for the mental block fires. The athlete can't perform a skill they can normally do in their sleep. The sooner we can get to work on the block, the easier it is to resolve. Mental blocks that have lasted weeks or months are usually easy to take care of. Mental blocks that have lasted years are much tougher to work with because the imprinting in the brain and the body has gone on for so long.

Last, it's some combination of everything I have mentioned. They could have a bad fall. They could have a lot of stressors going on in their life *and* they could have a high stress event. I work with kids whose parents are divorced.

The divorce kicked in the mental tumbling block. Or, like I said, a bad car wreck, an injury or overload at school.

I have one girl who came to see me for a mental block. Her major stressor was finding out that her grandmother had cancer. I know these are issues that are not related to sports, but they are a part of the stress response that keeps adding stress to the scale and eventually the scale tips and the mental block kicks in.

Is this complicated? Yeah. Is it tragic for these athletes? Absolutely. Is it embarrassing for them sometimes? Yes. Things not to do: Don't punish the behavior. Don't kick them out of the gym. Don't make them climb ropes. Don't make them run. Don't call them out in front of people, parents, coaches and teammates. Be empathetic and understanding. It's not that they don't want to do well; their brain won't let them do it. So, you have to guide them through this process. You've got to help them find the resources they need to get through. Laughing at them and humiliating them doesn't work. It only makes the imprinting worse. Now they are adding you, the negative humiliating coach, parent or teammate to the list of stressors that are causing the mental block. You are now part of the problem.

Do you want to be part of the problem? Or do you want to be part of the solution? Mental blocks are tough on everyone in the athlete's system, not just the athlete. It's a very complex issue for athletes to overcome. But I hope that this information will help you understand that it's not something they're doing on purpose. It's not something that they're doing because they're lazy. It's not something they're doing because they don't care. It's because their brain is actually doing its job. It has made misperceptions about some critical events in their lives. The brain has wired things up in a counterproductive way. Nonetheless the brain is doing what it thinks it's supposed to be doing to keep the athlete safe or keep them out of harm's way.

So, identifying falls, stressors, triggers, past experiences, and creating a safe, calm environment is the key. Once we get them through the mental blocks, I get these wonderful videos from the athlete. They are now doing the very skill they did when they got hurt, or had the fall, or the injury, or the accident. They have resolved conflicts, or dealt with whatever caused the block originally, and they're out tumbling again, doing back flips and jumping off people's shoulders.

One last point--where the mind leads the body follows. If an athlete has a mental block, it is almost certain that they are focusing their mind on stressful, fear based, anxiety producing thoughts and images. The limbic system sees what they see; it thinks what they think; it feels what they feel; and it perceives what they perceive. Fear-based, and negative thinking play a huge role in mental blocks. I always tell athletes "if we can see it we can be it." This is true for the scary, frightening and embarrassing things they focus on too. If they charge these negative thoughts and images up with intense negative emotion, they are producing an imprint that the brain perceives as threatening. If the brain perceives a threat it will shut down the athlete's ability to perform what has been easy and natural in the past.

We just worked our way through the section on mental blocks in sports. The next segment is going to look at the common traits of championship teams and cultures.

CHAMPIONSHIP TEAM CULTURE

"There are only two options regarding commitment. You're either In or you're OUT. There is no such thing as life in between."

Pat Riley

Alright! I'm excited to share this information because I put a lot of work into this. Not that I haven't put a lot of work into the other areas, but this topic is really special because I have taken information from interviews that I have done with NBA players, NFL players, MLB players and Champion's from other sports. I've gone back 40 years, 20 years, 7 years, 5 years, and you know what, the information is the same no matter whom I interviewed. Teams that achieve the highest level of greatness in their sport are doing the same things. I got the same answer from every single athlete when I asked the questions about what their teams did to win it all. I asked NBA Hall of Famers for five minutes of their time, and I had remarkable 45-minute conversations with each of them because they were all excited to talk about it. We didn't talk about stats, wins, how many block shots they had, what their free throw percentage was, how many field goals they kicked or how many home runs they hit in the World Series. We didn't talk about that. We talked about their team, their heart, their character, their relationships and so many other fascinating contributors to success at the highest levels in sports. I'm going to share with you what I have learned, step by step. These powerful concepts are the corner stories of a winning sports culture.

High Level of Buy In!

The first thing they told me or the first common theme that I heard from each of these athletes was, "We all had a very high level of buy in." They all bought into the plan at an extremely high level. They committed to the leadership plan, to the greater good of what this team was all about and to the dream of winning a championship and being the best.

Whether it had to do with running a specific play, the way they practiced, developing culture in the locker room and on and off the field, wherever that might be, they all bought in at a remarkably high level. Everybody on the team bought in. There were no rogue athletes. That doesn't mean you can't win championships with rogue athletes, but the ones that enjoyed this process the most, had everybody buying in at a very high level. The rogue athletes eventually moved on or were released because they didn't buy into the plan and the goals of the team and organization. They tended to be a distraction, and championship teams don't have many distractions.

Coachable Athletes

All the athletes I interviewed said they were coachable. They all followed their coach's leadership. They had coaches who brought the best out of them, who respected their personality and what they brought to the team and to the game. They worked their tails off for these coaches to be the best, to achieve the goals that they set for themselves.

Personal Responsibility

Athletes on championship teams had a very high level of

responsibility for their role on the team. Whether their role was to be a special team player, the 6th, 7th or 8th player off the bench, or the middle relief pitcher, they all took a very high level of pride and personal responsibility in that role.

They also took responsibility for their behaviors away from their respective sport. They took good care of themselves and made sure they were not a distraction to the team.

Toughness and Togetherness

The next thing I heard from these athletes really made a lot of sense to me. They all said that the tougher things got, the more together they came as a team. Teams that aren't championship teams tend to fall apart at crunch time. When the pressure is at its highest, when every shot counts, when they desperately need a defensive stop, the cracks in their foundation are exposed and they struggle at critical times of competition. If there are flaws in the culture, flaws in the foundation and if there are egos involved, then there will be weakness in the system.

Those cracks show up during crunch time. When the pressure is at its highest, that will be the time when teams fall apart. When you have a championship team, the tougher things get, the stronger the team comes together, the more fortified and the stronger the foundation.

I interviewed Kevin McHale, NBA Hall of Fame, NBA Top 50 All Time, and NBA Champion with the Boston Celtics. He said his teams focused on "toughness and togetherness." The more solid the foundation, the more they can weather adversity. They can handle a player going down with an injury. Somebody else will step in and perform remarkably well. They might have lost the first game on their home court, or they might have almost gotten beat or they might have blown a lead in the fourth quarter. From that event they rallied, they came together and they were much tougher and closer, more together, because of those experiences.

Team Closeness

They also told me, that they had a very high level of closeness. They hang out together on and off the court, in and away from their sport. They spend time together. They would do things that everybody liked to do. If someone had a favorite restaurant, they might go to that guy's restaurant, then go over to somebody else's house for movie night, or hang out, or play videogames together. They have competition as a team on road trips and things like that. They just hang out together and when they hang out together, they talk a lot about each other.

They get to know each other.

They are vulnerable with each other. They learn about each other's lives and from that learning and growing, guess what? They learn to care a great deal about each other. They learn to really love and care and support each other and with that, it doesn't matter who has the success. If somebody got all the playing time one night, and another guy got just two minutes, or another guy only got a couple of at bats in the game, it didn't matter, the team won. They all bought into the greater good. They were successful; they were winners. Everyone was happy.

Someone else might have the limelight one night and the next night they might score only five points. It just didn't matter. They are winning. They are together, and they are having a great time as a team.

Accountability

championship teams have very strong and vocal leadership around accountability. Accountability is one of the cornerstones of a great sports culture. If you don't have accountability, it becomes about individual need. There's an absence of trust. No one knows how to work through conflict. Things become lax. There's no adherence to the rules and guidelines of that organization, that culture. And then it becomes all about me, me, me. Ego takes over and it becomes all about individual player stats or playing time.

I've seen that happen to professional and college teams. They have great years and then the culture begins to fall apart because there's no accountability. Vocal leadership around accountability and leadership keep the players in line. With championship teams, strong leadership keeps everything moving in the right direction. The individual players and the team are utilizing their energy and resources at a very high level. They handle ego, distractions and resolve issues. Accountability is better when it comes from the team leaders rather than the coaches. This frees coaches up to just coach, and it helps build trust and cohesiveness. Strong leadership within the team helps build a very strong foundation for the team to build their winning culture.

Work Through Conflict Quickly

Championship teams embrace and work through conflict.

If conflict comes up, they don't ignore it or sweep it under the rug. They deal with it with strong leadership. They have meetings. They sit down as a team and discuss and work through issues that affect team chemistry and cohesiveness. championship teams work through conflict and through using this process, they get closer. They know how to work through storms and get to the other side of the storm stronger and wiser.

Great teams learn how to storm. They are okay with the tension and discomfort that comes with conflict.

I have worked with teams where star players' lockers are next to each other and they don't talk to each other. I have been with teams where coaches are out of integrity and no one wants to hold them accountable because they are afraid of conflict. I have worked with teams where fear is used to hold everyone in check and players are afraid to speak up for fear of losing their place on the team. Each of these teams never met their full potential because they didn't know how or weren't allowed to have conflict and accountability.

They Learned from Conflict Quickly

Not only do championship teams know how to do conflict, they learn very quickly from conflict. They don't make the same mistakes repeatedly. They learn from it and move on. They work through the conflict quickly and learn quickly. They learn how to recognize when similar issues are surfacing and take care of them before they become distractions again.

They Support Each Other

They're very supportive of each other. Older players mentor younger players, bring them along, bring them up to speed. They create an environment where it is okay for the younger players to make mistakes and learn from them. They understand that there are no mistakes, only learning. They celebrate the success. They celebrate everyone else's success. They are committed to do whatever it takes to win. They show up on time. They work their tails off and they are committed to the plan--a very high level of commitment. Older players, veterans, model these behaviors to the younger players. There is an atmosphere of expectation where everyone teaches, and learns from each other.

They Trust Each Other

They have a very high level of trust for each other. Trust comes from integrity, accountability and responsibility. You do what you say you're going to do. Your word can be honored and respected. Trust is the foundation of a great team. Without trust, as I said earlier, you can't work through conflict and everything begins to fall apart under stress and pressure. Great teams have a very high level of trust with each other.

They Understand They Need Each Other

Championship teams realize that they need each other, that they are a functioning unit and they need each other professionally. They also need each other personally. These friendships are valuable. They look forward to spending time together. They know they can depend on each other in certain situations in a game. There is a certain sense of trust and knowing that their teammates will be there for them. They also know they need each other away from their sport, in their everyday life.

Tremendous Pride

Players on championship teams take a lot of pride in playing the game at a very high level. Hakeem Olajuwon, NBA Hall of Fame, Top 50 All Time Player, NBA Champion with the Houston Rockets said, "We played honest basketball." And I thought that was such an awesome way to put it. "We played honest basketball." Integrity, pride, responsibility for what we're doing is playing the game at the highest level. They had a tremendous amount of fun playing the game. They made it fun. They were in a culture that made playing the game fun.

I have worked with athletes that were miserable in their organizations, and they leave and go to another organization that has a winning culture and they're thriving. They are different players because they're able to expand themselves and open up that personality that we've talked about. They perform with passion, total engagement and a resounding commitment to excellence. They have a tremendous amount of fun playing the game, in and away from their respective sports.

Speaking of off the court, these champion athletes handle off-court issues very quickly. They don't let anyone get too far out of line. They bring them back in, and the ones that can't handle that, either don't play or they are asked to leave the organization, or they choose to leave. Sadly, you've seen stories like that where a team is on its way to greatness and some player falls by the wayside because they can't step up and have that high level of accountability that's required.

Love and passion for the game! Love and passion for each other! The last response that I thought was remarkable, "All of our energy was moving in the same direction." There wasn't interference around ego or conflicts. That means physical energy, mental, emotional and spiritual energy were all moving in the same direction very efficiently. They had a connection to each other. Their passion for the game. Their mental and emotional resources were all channeling their *physical* energy in the right direction. There were no energy drainers or energy leaks. They all channel their energy towards the common goal. Now this went back like I said to Champion's five years ago, seven years ago, 11 years ago and even 20 years ago.

What really interested me as I thought back, "Wow, it's been 40 some-odd years ago since I played on a state championship high school football team here in Texas." And you know what? Forty years ago, and I can say that everything these championship athletes said was true for a great championship high school team. Every one of them-- great coach's leadership and a high level of accountability. We loved each other and still love each other to this day. We were supportive and happy for everyone else's success. We had a lot of fun, worked through conflict, connected on and off the field and resolved issues that were creating energy drains. Our energy focused on our common goal of winning a state championship. We trusted each other. We knew we needed each other. We took pride in what we were doing out there on the field. We all had a very high level of responsibility for our roles on the team.

My research has revealed, it's a proven formula for success. If your teams aren't doing this, you might need to sit down and take a good hard look at your culture and what it is that you're doing that's preventing your team from buying into this proven formula for success.

In Closing and Thank You

I hope you've enjoyed these concepts, tools and techniques that I have put together in the Champion's Mental Edge. I hope the stories helped drive home the key points I have made in this book. They are an accumulation of a lifetime of experiences, knowledge, struggles, research and passion. I am grateful to be able to share them with you. If you find value in it, share it with other people. I am certain there are people out there, that you know, who could benefit from any of the topics that I covered. If something in the information has touched you, if something lit a fire in you, or you recognize that there is an area in your game that you need to improve, feel free to contact me.

There's more work we can do. Tell me a little bit about you. What's your sport? What's your passion? What's going on and how can I help you, your team or your organization. Let's take this to the next level.

ROBERT ANDREWS

ABOUT THE AUTHOR

Robert Andrews is a mental training expert and Founder and Director of The Institute of Sports Performance in Houston, TX.

He has been in private practice as a sports performance consultant and licensed therapist for 22 years.

In the 2016 Rio Olympics, Robert worked with multiple Gold, Silver and Bronze Medalists in swimming and gymnastics. He attended the 2008 Beijing and 2012 London Olympic games where he worked with U.S.A. and international athletes in gymnastics, trampoline, and track & field.

Locally he works with the Houston Texans, and local universities, and has been a consultant for the Houston Astros and Houston Rockets. His passion is working with athletes, teams and sports cultures, as they strive to reach peak athletic potential and create healthy and empowering sports cultures.

Robert is an expert at assisting injured athletes in overcoming the mental and emotional impact of their sports related injury.

Robert also works with coaches, teams, and organizations.

He is married and has two kids. His wife Gisele was a standout volleyball player. His son Galen played college baseball, and his daughter Abby plays high school and club volleyball. Robert maintains an active and balanced lifestyle that promotes all around mental, emotional, physical, and spiritual health and wellbeing.

Robert's contact information.

Robert B. Andrews
3701 Kirby Dr. Suite 713
Houston, TX 77098

Office: 713 522 2200
Website: www.tinssp.com
Email: robertandrews@tinssp.com
Champion's Mental Edge Performance
Program: http://www.championsmentaledge.com/